THE
MAKING OF AMERICA
SERIES

FREEHOLD
A HOMETOWN HISTORY

FREEHOLD HIGH SCHOOL BASEBALL TEAM, 1922. *This picture was taken on Mrs. Parker's porch. Her house was on Hudson Street next to the high school, which was on the corner of Hudson and Bennett Streets. These streets were both named in honor of Mr. Hudson Bennett, a prominent citizen of Freehold who owned the land in this area when it was farm land. From left to right are: (first row) Meyer Foosaner, John MacMurtrie, Gilday Freeman, Edward King, Wesley Walling; (second row) Coach H. John Witman, Aloysius Carey, Clifford T. Burke, George Quinn, Warren McChesney; (third row) Charles McCue, and Brandt Davis. (Courtesy Ira C. Tilton.)*

THE
MAKING OF AMERICA
SERIES

FREEHOLD
A HOMETOWN HISTORY

BARBARA PEPE

ARCADIA

Published by Arcadia Publishing,
an imprint of Tempus Publishing, Inc.
2 Cumberland Street
Charleston, SC 29401

Printed in Great Britain.

Library of Congress Catalog Card Number: 2002116805

For all general information contact Arcadia Publishing at:
Telephone 843-853-2070
Fax 843-853-0044
E-Mail sales@arcadiapublishing.com

For customer service and orders:
Toll-Free 1-888-313-2665

Visit us on the Internet at http://www.arcadiapublishing.com

Front cover: One of the most exciting meets in harness racing took place on October 3, 1953 at Freehold Raceway. Three horses: Patchover, Penny Maid, and Payne Hall won the race in a triple dead heat. The three winners are pictured here with their drivers in front of the original grandstand.

CONTENTS

ACKNOWLEDGMENTS

There are several people who I want to acknowledge for their help and support during the course of the year that it took to research and write this book. The Monmouth County Historical Association holds a treasure chest of information and, if not for the assistance of Carla Tobias and Megan Springate, I would not have been able to find some of the buried treasure. A special thanks to Lee Ellen Griffith for permitting me to use photos from MCHA's collection. Nancy DuBois Wood is a walking encyclopedia of Freehold history and was especially helpful with tying up loose ends and reading sections of the manuscript. Rich Walling was a wealth of information on the Battle of Monmouth and Professor Rich Veit lent a critical eye to the chapter on the Lenni Lenape. In my search for photos and images, Barbara Greenberg from the Freehold Public Library was more than generous in sharing the library's collection, as was Don Bielak from Freehold Raceway. Randall Gabrielan and Carl Beams both shared their private collections with me. Thank you to my good friend Kat Veneziano, for listening to me moan and groan when things got tough and for reading several chapters of the manuscript. It would be impossible to list all my family members, but you know who you are and I want to thank you for believing in me and for supporting me through my academic and literary endeavors. Last, but not least, I dedicate this book to my son Richard, who is forever in my heart.

INTRODUCTION

Freehold, New Jersey has grown from an area that was sparsely inhabited by the Lenni Lenape Indians to a vital residential and commercial community of over 30,000 people. This thriving county seat is located in the heart of New Jersey at the center of Monmouth, one of New Jersey's original counties. When Freehold was created on March 7, 1683, the county encompassed present-day Monmouth County, plus what is known today as Ocean County, and parts of Burlington County. Today's Monmouth County spans an area of 665 square miles stretching from the Atlantic Ocean to the interior of the state about 10 miles from Trenton, the state capital. Its coastline runs along the eastern part of the state from Raritan Bay, around Sandy Hook, and southward along the Atlantic Ocean to the Manasquan Inlet—the dividing line between Monmouth and Ocean Counties. Monmouth County's coastline has a total of 27 oceanfront miles and 26 bayfront miles.

Freehold covers an area of about 39 square miles. The topography is characterized by rolling hills and lowlands. To the east of Freehold lie the Mount Pleasant Hills, which reach elevations of 200-380 feet. To the west are the Hominy Hills, which range from 200-307 feet. Freehold itself is mostly a lowland area lying between these hills, making it suitable for farming.

Freehold has a unique municipal structure in that it consists of two distinct municipalities with different forms of government: the borough and the township. The township surrounds the borough. If you were to ask a resident of either municipality where they live, the answer would be "Freehold." Although both entities are recognized by a common name, their respective forms of government—as well as their boundary lines—distinguish them.

The development of Freehold has been a process spanning almost 300 years. By the end of the seventeenth century, New Jersey had been organized and divided into East and West Jersey. The General Assembly of East Jersey created four counties, one of which was Monmouth. A decade later, Monmouth County was subdivided into three townships, including Freehold. Originally formed as a township, Freehold experienced changes in its political structure and geographic boundaries between 1693 and 1926. Those changes laid the foundation for Freehold Borough and Freehold Township as they exist today.

One of the more significant events in Freehold's history was the 1713 decision to move the county seat from Shrewsbury to Freehold. From 1715 until 1798, Freehold was known as Monmouth Court House. It was the judicial center, as well as the hub of agricultural, commercial, and political activity. Many debts were settled in the rooms of the courthouse. People served time for crimes such as horse thievery and battery in the jail that was part of the building. The Declaration of Independence was read to locals from the steps of the courthouse shortly after Thomas Jefferson wrote it in Philadelphia. The structure was also the meeting place where Patriots gathered to protest the tyrannical acts of King George III and to hear news of the American Revolution from throughout the colonies. One of the bloodiest, most horrendous battles of the American Revolution, the Battle of Monmouth, took place in Monmouth Court House. It was on the courthouse steps that residents of Monmouth County met and drew up a petition demanding that General George Washington seek revenge for the capture and death of Captain Joshua Huddy, an incident that led the infant country into its first international conflict.

In the middle of the nineteenth century, as the United States headed towards and fought the Civil War, Freehold experienced its own division. Prompted by a legislative act, several towns broke away and formed independent municipalities. The actual division of Freehold into a township and a borough took place on July 5, 1919, when parts of the township and parts of what remained of the town united as a borough. A final section of the township joined the borough on September 7, 1926, completing the division of Freehold. Today, Freehold Township and Freehold Borough exist as independent municipalities whose histories share the same roots.

As the boundaries and political structure of Freehold changed in the late nineteenth and early twentieth centuries, so did its culture. Changes in commercial activities brought on by the Industrial Revolution quickened and improved agricultural and manufacturing processes. The arrival of the railroad opened new markets for produce and manufactured items. There was more leisure time as people were not quite as burdened with the chores of production. Residential development boomed during the late twentieth century, mostly in the Township, and continues today. Along with agricultural, commercial, transportation, and residential development came the need for more schools, places of worship, and leisure time activities. Freehold met those needs.

Freehold is currently undergoing a revitalization and expansion of the business district located in the heart of the borough. Freehold Township began as an agricultural area and survived geographic division, commercial evolution, and political structure changes. Today, the main commercial activities are centered at Freehold Raceway Mall and extend along Routes 9, 33, and 537. Residential development includes amenities that make the township a prime family-oriented living area. In spite of the development, 25 percent of the total area of the township and borough is dedicated to open space. This helps the township and borough remain prime areas for commerce, leisure activities, and family life.

Freehold of the twenty-first century has been reduced in size from colonial times. Its political structure has changed since its creation, but Freehold has not lost its significance to New Jersey. The 1.9-square-mile borough serves as the county seat for one of New Jersey's largest counties. Freehold Borough is home to Freehold Raceway, the oldest pari-mutuel harness race track in the United States. It is also proud to be the birthplace of rock 'n' roll singer and songwriter Bruce Springsteen.

This book tells the story of the people who shaped Freehold, from the Native American Lenni Lenape to the modern-day citizens whose lives are the essence of what makes Freehold an enormously popular place to live and a thriving community. People are the heart and soul of America, and the people of Freehold have created and continue to create a town in which they can confidently exclaim, "Proud to be American."

A&M KARAGHUESIAN RUG MILL. This aerial view shows a different perspective of the rug mill and its surrounding area before 1950. (Courtesy of Monmouth County Historical Association Library and Archives.)

1. Land of the Lenni Lenape

Before Freehold Borough was incorporated, before Freehold Township came into being, and before the Scottish, English, Dutch, and other settlers colonized New Jersey, a group of Native Americans lived in the area. They were known as the Lenni Lenape, although later English-speaking people called them the Delaware tribe after the river along whose banks they lived. American historians loosely translate their name to mean "people of the land," while the Algonquin-speaking Lenape translate it to either "original people" or "true men." The Delaware were a part of the Algonquin Nation, which also included the Iroquois tribe. Their ancestors had emigrated from the cold, harsh, northwestern section of the continent. According to Lenape tradition, they migrated east and south in search of an area that would supply food and a suitable climate. Their trek ended on the eastern shores of North America, including the area that became New Jersey. They lived in independent villages with no central political authority and did not consider themselves a unified tribe. The Lenni Lenape numbered about 100,000 by the time European explorers arrived on the shores of America. They resided in the northern and central parts of New Jersey, including the area known today as Freehold.

Archaeologists have found evidence of the Lenni Lenape civilization dating back to c. 10,000 B.C. The tribe was able to adapt to the natural landscape of New Jersey, with all its seasonal changes, and lived in harmony with the land for centuries. The area provided a plentiful source of deer, bear, small game, fowl, nuts, and berries—the main components of the tribe's diet. The Atlantic Ocean was abundant with clams, oysters, and fish—the last also being in great supply in numerous lakes, rivers, and streams. Although the Lenape were primarily hunters and gatherers, the rich soil was suitable for growing grain and vegetables, and some practiced farming. Lenape women were solely responsible for the farms, whose fields covered areas as large as 200 acres. They produced such crops as corn, beans, sweet potatoes, and tobacco.

Some archaeologists argue that the Lenape lived a nomadic life. During the warmer months of summer, they moved to the coastal region, where they camped and enjoyed the bountiful seafood from the Atlantic Ocean. The colder winter months found them in the inland areas of the state, where hunting provided their

LENNI LENAPE LONGHOUSE. The Native American Lenni Lenape lived in structures such as this longhouse. This replica was constructed at a Pow Wow held in Sandy Hook, New Jersey in 1997.

staple food supply along with hides used to make clothing. Archaeological evidence supports the Lenape living in temporary buildings, situated about 6 to 10 miles apart. Such rock shelters, windbreaks, and lodges were built with stone tools from saplings and bark. Temporary shelters would be consistent with a nomadic lifestyle. In summer months, a simple tent made from deer hide would provide sufficient protection from the heat and sun. In colder months, however, a more substantial dwelling would be needed as shelter from the very frigid northern winter.

In addition to archaeological evidence, some written works describe these original New Jersey inhabitants. The September 4, 1609 entry in the log book of Henry Hudson's ship *Half Moon* refers to the Native Americans encountered by Hudson and his crew:

> This day the people of the country came aboard of us and seemed very glad of our coming, and brought green tobacco leaves and gave us of it for knives and beads. They go in deerskins, loose and well dressed. They have yellow copper. They desire clothes and are very civil. They have a great store of maize or Indian wheat, whereof they make good bread.

In the early centuries of their inhabitation of New Jersey, the Lenape's main causes of death were starvation and exposure to the cold winter climate, but

European settlers brought far more destructive forces in the seventeenth and eighteenth centuries. The Dutch, English, and Scottish helped improve the Lenape's survival techniques, but also introduced diseases—such as small pox, measles, and influenza—that destroyed much of the native population. While the number of Lenapes slowly decreased, the number of colonists settling in New Jersey steadily increased. The Dutch established the colony of New Netherlands along Manhattan's southern border. Some moved across the Hudson River into the peninsula that is present-day New Jersey. While most settled in the northern part of the peninsula, some ventured south and inland to set up trading posts. The interior of the peninsula proved to be a rich and profitable farmland; the business of agriculture took root and thrived.

The Lenape were slowly forced off their beloved Lenapehoking (Land of the Lenape), as they did not have a concept of land ownership. European settlers rationalized taking the Native Americans' land by virtue of a sovereign grant. The Europeans who migrated to America in order to escape oppression did not realize the irony of their actions in the new world; in their quest for freedom, they failed to realize their impact on the freedom of the native people. As more colonists settled in New Jersey, more Lenapes were forced into Pennsylvania, Ohio, Indiana, Missouri, Kansas, Texas, and Oklahoma. In some cases, their land was taken without any regard or remuneration. In other cases, the settlers struck

LENNI LENAPE CANOE. *The Lenni Lenape dug out red cedar trees to make canoes used for fishing and traveling through the waters of New Jersey.*

bargains and purchased the land for ridiculously paltry amounts of money or trade items. Only a small number of Lenape remained in New Jersey by 1749. In April of that year, Governor Jonathan Belcher acknowledged that there were only about 60 Lenape families in the eastern part of the province.

In the eighteenth century, reservations were established for Native Americans, including one at Brotherton in Burlington County in 1758. By 1802, the colonial government purchased the land upon which the reservation was situated. Some of the remaining Lenape moved first to New Stockbridge, near Oneida Lake, New York and then to Fox River, Wisconsin. Others moved to Pennsylvania and ultimately settled in Oklahoma. By 1832, only about 40 Lenape families remained in New Jersey. This small group petitioned the state for a settlement of $2,000 for their traditional fishing and hunting rights. They selected a tribal elder to represent them, Shawuskukhkung, whose name means "wilted grass," but who had adopted the Americanized name Bartholomew S. Calvin. He was a graduate of Princeton College and a veteran of the American Revolution. At 76 years old, he went before the state legislature and presented the petition. His words were sadly true:

BURLINGTON PATH. This driveway runs alongside the old Baptist Cemetery in Freehold Township. The deed to the adjacent property describes it as being located on the Burlington Path.

I am old and weak and poor, and therefore a fit representative of my people. You are young and strong and rich, and therefore fit representatives of your people. But let me beg you for a moment to lay aside the recollections of your strength and of our weakness that your minds may be prepared to examine with candor the subject of our claims.

The petition was granted. The Lenape received money for the rights, but virtually faded from New Jersey's collective memory.

Today, one of the only references to the Lenape regards the Burlington Path. In fact, one of the greatest contributions that the Lenape made to the state was a vast travel network. They used footpaths following the natural contours of the land, including ridges and watersheds. European settlers then used these numerous native trails as precursors to today's modern road system. As time went on, the paths were widened to accommodate horses and wagons. Logs were laid across narrow streams and ferries crossed wider streams. Around 1684, a road was built from Perth Amboy to Burlington, the capitals of East and West Jersey. It connected people along the Delaware River near modern-day Camden to those along the Atlantic Coast near Highlands. It was known as the "Great Road," but was more commonly called the "Burlington Path." It followed a zigzag pattern from the Delaware River to the Atlantic Ocean, around ponds, along brooks and creeks, over hills, and through the pine forest of central New Jersey. Sometime in the mid-nineteenth century, roadways throughout New Jersey, including the Burlington Path, were realigned and straightened. By 1850, travelers called the roadway the Burlington old path. In 1796, the name was officially changed to Monmouth Road by an act of legislation. Today, Route 537 closely follows its direction, but very little remains of the original Indian trail. Still, every now and then a local may refer to the road as the former Burlington Path.

The "people of the land" who dwelled in the area of Freehold for thousands of years have been replaced by another group of people who arrived on its shores fewer than 500 years ago. These people and their descendants developed the area's fertile soil into an agricultural center. During the Revolutionary War, they formed a colonial militia with better weapons than the natives possessed. They survived major wars, an industrial revolution, and many social and political changes. They were instrumental in the evolution of Freehold from a pastoral landscape to a booming residential and commercial center of the twenty-first century.

2. COLONIAL FREEHOLD AND A NEW MUNICIPALITY

Freehold was officially recognized as a township in 1693, but the area was known by that name as it developed throughout the seventeenth century. From settlement days up through modern times, Freehold has been known for its farms and for raising horses. Early farms produced a variety of crops such as potatoes, beans, corn, and rye. Later, with the advent of the industrial revolution and improvements to farm machinery, farmers became more specialized and produced only one or two cash crops, operated dairy farms, or raised livestock. At the advent of the seventeenth century, the Dutch hold in the new world was growing with settlements in New Netherlands (New York) and on the peninsula of New Jersey. By mid-century, they were a formidable force in the new world. They had developed a system of trading with the Native Americans using their many existing trails. Although at times the trading was unscrupulous, it proved to be very profitable for the Dutch.

The old Indian trail, known in the early seventeenth century as the Burlington Path and late seventeenth century as King's Highway, became an integral part of the Dutch trade network. There were two main branches of the path. One passed through the area known today as Freehold, then took a northerly direction through what would become Middletown Township, where it connected to another trail known as the Minisink Path. (The Minisink Path ran from Middletown northward through northern New Jersey.) The other main branch of the Burlington Path passed through Freehold and continued in a northeasterly direction to Long Branch on the Atlantic shore. There were also several other smaller arteries leading to the shore. The Burlington Path was crucial to commerce in the new world because it provided a known, tried-and-true route traversing critical centers of commerce in New Jersey.

While the Dutch were doing well in their trading business in the new world and becoming able and industrious farmers, the British were fighting a civil war. That war lasted from 1640 to 1660 and when it was over, England searched for ways to strengthen its position as a colonial force. In order to do so, England needed to increase its wealth; the new world provided a perfect opportunity to do so. Colonial America's proximity to the Atlantic coast made it a superb center for commerce. England saw the new world as a means to becoming the richest and most powerful country on earth.

There were also a large number of Scottish Quakers and Presbyterians looking for a place to escape religious persecution. Some voluntarily traveled thousands of miles across the Atlantic to start their new lives, while others were banished from their homeland and sent to the new world, where it was expected they would perish. These people were mostly farmers who were not necessarily interested in striking it rich or developing trade with the new world. They simply wanted to live an agrarian life while following their faith. The area that would become known as New Jersey provided a prime piece of real estate for farming in an environment that afforded the settlers religious freedom. The area known as Freehold was especially inviting to the Scots, with its rich soil and temperate climate providing excellent conditions for farming.

The people who came to the new world—whether voluntarily or by banishment—were truly pioneers. They ventured into an unknown world and had to make due with the conditions found upon arrival. There were no service establishments, no paved nor marked roads, no institutions of learning, and no churches in their new home. They immediately had to become self-sufficient. They set up their homesteads wherever they found a suitable spot of land, built their own homes, and provided their own food and materials for survival. Before long, however, King Charles II of England began staking claims in the new world.

On March 12, 1664, King Charles granted the land between the Delaware and Connecticut Rivers to his brother James, Duke of York. A large portion of this tract eventually became the states of New York and New Jersey. At the time that Charles granted this land, it was sparsely populated by Dutch, Scottish, and English settlers. Two months later, James sent his friend Richard Nicolls to his newly-acquired estate. Nicolls was appointed proprietary governor with the instructions to usurp power from the Dutch. Knowing how successful the Dutch had been in establishing trade in the new world, James intended to prove to his brother Charles that the colonies could be profitable to England as well.

As governor, Nicolls aggressively took charge of the colony. His actions became part of an ongoing anti-proprietary movement that pitted the king's appointees against those appointed by the Duke of York. Nicolls granted two tracts of land to a group of Quakers and Baptists. The first tract was located between the Raritan and Passaic Rivers in present-day Essex County. The second tract encompassed the land along the shore from Sandy Hook to Barnegat Bay and 25 miles up the Raritan River in present-day Monmouth and Ocean Counties. (The area that would become Freehold was situated on the latter tract of land.) Unfortunately, Nicolls did not have the authority to grant land. Such a privilege was vested only in the king or James, who had been granted the land by the king. The problem was exacerbated when James simultaneously rewarded the loyalty of his two friends, Lord John Berkeley and Sir George Carteret, with a proprietary grant later in 1664. James's appointees then sent Philip Carteret, a 26-year-old cousin of Sir

MONMOUTH COUNTY COURTHOUSE, c. 1770. This drawing depicts an artist's view of the courthouse as it was around 1770. (Courtesy of Freehold Public Library.)

George, to the colony in 1665 to act as governor. Nicolls was outraged and responded by resigning.

To further complicate matters, Lord Berkeley lost interest in New Jersey and sold his portion in 1676 to two Quakers, Major John Fenwick and Edward Byllynge, for a mere £1,000. Sir George Carteret—who still owned his share of the land that had been properly granted by James—did not agree with Fenwick and Byllynge, so they decided to divide New Jersey into East and West. Philip Carteret remained governor of East Jersey until 1682, while Fenwick and Byllynge retained jurisdiction over West Jersey. Byllynge went on to serve as governor of West Jersey from 1680 to 1687.

Prior to the division of New Jersey, James had determined the northern boundary of the land granted to Berkeley and Carteret by drawing a line from the upper Delaware River at 41° 40' north latitude to the Hudson River. This line has been the northern boundary of New Jersey ever since. The 7,500-square-mile tract of land extended from this line to the southern tip of the peninsula that lay between the Atlantic Ocean and the Delaware River. The division of East and West Jersey was subsequently marked by a line that ran from Little Egg Harbor to the original northern boundary line. Not until 1687 was an official survey of the province line completed by a Scot named George Keith.

George Keith was a native of Aberdeen, Scotland, born *c.* 1638. He studied to be a Presbyterian minister in the mid-1650s, but due to differences between him and the Presbytery, he became a Quaker in 1662. In the 1660s, Keith was imprisoned several times for his radical preaching. On July 31, 1684, he was appointed surveyor general to the Council of Proprietors of the province of East Jersey. He set off for America and arrived some time during the spring of the following year. Keith lived on a plantation in Freehold until 1689, when he moved to Pennsylvania. He remained in the states until 1693 and then returned to London with his family, where he died in 1715.

In 1687, Keith was given the task of surveying the boundaries of the province line between East and West Jersey. The line started at Little Egg Harbor on the southeastern coast and ran in a northwesterly direction to the Raritan River in Somerset County. It then passed through southern Monmouth County, which was sparsely populated at the time. It continued to the east of Crosswicks, west of Allentown, and slightly west of Princeton. Freehold, founded in 1693, was clearly located in the province of East Jersey. Keith's province line remained the boundary until 1743, when John Lawrence was commissioned by the East Jersey proprietors to resurvey the line.

Lawrence worked on the survey between September and October. His line started at the same point as Keith's, but moved slightly to the east of that line. Unlike Keith, Lawrence determined the province line to be east of Allentown and Princeton, continue past the Raritan River in Somerset County and into Sussex County, and end at the Delaware River southwest of Dingman's Creek. Not until some time after 1769 did West Jersey officially recognize Lawrence's line. This province line ran fairly close to the boundary of Freehold, but both the 1687 and 1743 lines ran to the west of Freehold, making it part of East Jersey.

As the American colonies continued to take shape, new towns, cities, and counties were created. Freehold had not yet been designated as a township when, on March 7, 1683, the governor and council of East Jersey met and drew up a bill called *An Act to divide the Province into Four Counties.* This act created Essex, Bergen, Middlesex, and Monmouth Counties. The name Monmouth is believed to derive from Monmouthshire, England, the birthplace of Colonel Lewis Morris, who would become the first governor of New Jersey in 1738. Lewis had set up a plantation in Monmouth, which he called Tintern (and which later became Tinton Falls) after his family estate in Monmouthshire, England.

The provinces of East and West Jersey continued to flourish. Then, between October 12 and November 3, 1693, the general assembly of East Jersey met at Perth Amboy and passed legislation to subdivide Monmouth County into three townships: Shrewsbury, Middletown, and Freehold. Freehold was officially designated as a township by virtue of this subdivision, which was dated October 31, 1693. The minutes of the general assembly proceedings on that day give a brief boundary description of the newly designated township:

MONMOUTH COUNTY COURTHOUSE, c. 1731–1806. After fire destroyed the 1719 courthouse, this structure replaced it. (Courtesy of Monmouth County Historical Association Library and Archives.)

> The township of Freehold includes all the land from the head of Cheesequakes Creek, and runs along the lines of Middletown to Burlington Path; then along the line of Shrewsbury to the line of the Province; thence along the Province line to the line of the County; thence northeast along the said county line to where it began.

In 1693, the term "township" referred to the geographic delineation of a town. These delineations were sketchy at first, but eventually, the townships were surveyed and official boundary lines established. Freehold was surveyed and laid out as a geographic township sometime after 1708.

During the eighteenth century, municipal forms of government evolved. The Township Act of 1798 established the township form of municipal government as consisting of a specified number of committee members, one of whom would be selected to serve as mayor for one year. This was the only form of government that allowed the mayor to be selected by other committee members, rather than by voters in the community. As a result of the Township Act, Freehold incorporated as Freehold Township on February 21, 1798. The new municipality evolved and developed over the next 120 years before Freehold Borough organized as a separate entity and incorporated in 1919. In the twenty-first century, there are five members elected to the Freehold Township Committee who serve staggered three-year terms. The committee elects one member to serve as mayor and one as deputy mayor.

Freehold developed much like other communities in Monmouth County: dispersed farmsteads surrounded a cluster of homes that were situated around a central building, such as a tavern or a mill. In the case of Freehold, that central building was the courthouse. A courthouse and jail were initially located in Shrewsbury Township, which served as the county seat for Monmouth. But as the eighteenth century progressed, the county population increased and spread south and southwest. County leaders realized the need for a more central location to accommodate the expanding population and explored moving the courthouse and jail to either Middletown or Freehold. Middletown was north of Shrewsbury and too far from the rest of the county, which stretched far south and included present-day Ocean County and a small portion of present-day Burlington County. Freehold was more centrally located, so it was preferred as the new county seat. After much discussion during the 1713 session of the New Jersey General Assembly, an act was passed to establish an official courthouse in Freehold Township—the first step in moving the county seat from Shrewsbury to Freehold.

The members of the general assembly agreed that the courthouse should be constructed in a central location. Several Freehold property owners had suitable land. Two of those were John Okeson and John Reid. Okeson owned a tavern on the principal route of travel through Freehold, the Burlington Path. It was

MONMOUTH COUNTY COURTHOUSE, c. 1806. This structure replaced the one built in 1731. (Courtesy of Monmouth County Historical Association Library and Archives.)

suggested that the county purchase a portion of his property located on the southeast side of Main Street. Reid was an enterprising farmer with a vision for his own future. In March 1714, knowing that the township was searching for a central location for its new courthouse, he purchased a parcel of land from Thomas Combs. This land was also situated on the Burlington Path (present-day Main Street). It was less than an acre, but proved to be the perfect location for the new courthouse. On August 26th, five months after he purchased the property from Combs, Reid sold a small piece of the land to the Monmouth County Freeholders for the sum of 30 shillings. By eighteenth-century economic standards, this was a very modest sum. Reid, however, knew that once the new courthouse was built, the remainder of his property would increase in value.

In 1715, a courthouse and jail were built on this property (on the corner of present-day East Main and South Streets), the courts and jail were moved from Shrewsbury, and Freehold officially became the new county seat. At this point, Freehold Township became known as Monmouth Court House, and was known as such until 1795, when a post office was established.

There are no documents that show what the 1715 courthouse building looked like, but there is evidence that it was not effective as a jail. The *New Jersey Gazette* reported that two prisoners managed to escape shortly after the structure's construction. In response, it was rebuilt four years later in 1719. The only description that remains of this second structure is that it was a small wooden building. It stood until it was completely destroyed by fire sometime in 1727. Although there is no record of the exact date of the fire, the Monmouth County Quarter Sessions Minutes of January 28, 1728 contain a very descriptive report:

> At the Courts of Sessions & Pleas held at Freehold in and for the County of Monmouth in the month of January in the 2nd year of his majesties reign and since the last Courts of Sessions & Pleas held for this county the Court House having been burnt down, Henry Leonard, Esq. one of the judges of this court and one of the justices to which John Throckmorton and William Leeds, Esq's. two of the assistants of the said courts and also justices went together to the spot of ground whereupon the old Court House stood and there being attended by the Clerk of the Peace opened the Courts of Sessions & Pleas and immediately adjourned the same to the house of William Nichols, Esq.

The Courts of Sessions and Pleas, which heard cases relating to land and people's individual rights, managed as best they could in the Nichols residence, while the courthouse was rebuilt. The design and construction of the subsequent structure took several years to complete. By 1731, it opened and the business of the courts resumed a more normal schedule. This third courthouse continued to serve the county seat for nearly 75 years, through key events of the eighteenth century, particularly the American Revolution and the founding of the new nation. Then, between 1806 and 1808, construction began on the fourth courthouse in Freehold. When complete, it cost $28,000. This building was renovated and added on to several times over the next 50 years. Then, in the winter of 1855, a disastrous fire blazed through the courthouse.

Shortly after the fire was extinguished, a special meeting of the Board of Chosen Freeholders was called to consider the condition of the building. On Thursday, February 15, 1855 at 12:00 noon, they considered that the cause of the fire appeared to be suspicious. As noted in the minutes of this meeting, the actions of a female prisoner named Catharine Connor were the center of discussion. According to folklore, Connor was involved with setting the fire, although the accusation was not substantiated by the minutes of the Freeholders's meeting. They state only that her "condition" was considered by the Freeholders. What her condition was is not mentioned, so we are left to guess at what it might have been. In the minutes, Mr. Lefetra reported that Connor's state of health made it necessary to remove her from the "common cell at the jail" and place her in the "bedroom at the entrance of the jail." There is no account in the minutes of exactly how Catharine allegedly started this fire.

The minutes also report on some necessary decisions that allowed the Freeholders' business to continue while repairs were made to the damaged courthouse. They decided to rent the saloon on the corner of Throckmorton Avenue from A.H. Reid for $30 for the month of April. It was also agreed that, in addition to the necessary repairs, the courthouse would be enlarged to accommodate the increasing caseload and county offices.

MONMOUTH COUNTY COURTHOUSE, 1922. This is the courthouse as it appeared in 1922. (Courtesy of Monmouth County Historical Association Library and Archives.)

After the 1855 fire, there was some discussion amongst the Freeholders about the need for a fire engine and fire-fighting equipment. This issue had been brought up from time to time, but without urgency. The Freeholders decided to put off the decision again and to bring it up at the annual meeting in May. The discussion continued for another 10 years and in the meantime, two more fires damaged the courthouse: one on October 30, 1873 and one on April 19, 1930. These last two fires are discussed in detail later in the book.

In 1954, after four fires, the courthouse was moved from its original location on the Reid property and rebuilt two blocks north. The old courthouse located on present-day Main and Court Streets became known as the Hall of Records. In 2001, some of the county offices that were also housed in the old courthouse were moved out of the original Hall of Records to a newer, more secure, and fire-safe building at 33 Mechanic Street. Interestingly, one court room and judge's chambers still exist in the old courthouse because of a deed restriction made by John Reid in 1714. The stipulation requires that if the building ever ceases to be used as a courthouse, ownership reverts to the Reid family. Since direct descendants of John Reid still reside in Freehold Township, the Freeholders retain the one courtroom and chambers.

3. EARLY FAMILIES OF MONMOUTH COURT HOUSE

By the eighteenth century, Monmouth Court House was well on its way to becoming a cultural, social, and commercial center for Monmouth County. In 1708, an estimated 40 families inhabited the 30,000-acre township and about 40 more had settled in the outlying areas. By 1745, over half the residents of Freehold were Scottish immigrants. Descendants of these families still live in the area—some in their original homesteads, which have been preserved by historical organizations. Many of these early family names are memorialized on streets such as Applegate Road, Barkalow Avenue, Bowne Avenue, Brinckerhoff Avenue, Holmes Terrace, Rhea Street, Schanck Road, Thompson's Grove Road, and Throckmorton Street.

It would be impossible to tell the individual stories of the hundreds of early settlers, but several are worth mentioning because they are representative of the pluck and commitment characteristic of the majority. One of the earliest families to settle in Freehold were the Craigs from Scotland. John Craig Sr. (d. 1724), James, Archibald, and Ursula were the first members of the Craig family to arrive in New Jersey in 1685. They made their home in Perth Amboy for ten years. John Craig Sr. was an active member of the community and served in the general assembly. On June 11, 1690, he acquired a 150-acre farm on the south shore of the Raritan River in the area of Freehold Township known as Topanemus. He built a home there around 1710 and moved his family to this Freehold farm. John Craig Sr. died in 1724.

John's son Archibald purchased a piece of property in 1720 and also pursued the agrarian life. His property was located on what is currently the eastern border of Monmouth Battlefield State Park, just off Route 9 and Schibanoff Road. It is known today as the Craig House and is preserved and interpreted by the Friends of Monmouth Battlefield. The Craig farm remained in the family until the mid-twentieth century. In 1744, it passed from Archibald to his son Samuel, who built a 1 1/2-story Dutch frame house there in 1746. Upon Samuel's death, the property reverted to his father, whose will then left it to his son John Jr. Archibald died in 1751, when John Jr. was only 14 and not old enough to own real property.

So the Craig family rented the farm to tenants until John Jr. reached the age of 21 in 1758. He then took possession of the farm and added a 2-story Georgian-style addition to the west side of the home. The 200-acre farmstead also had a barn, barrack, corncrib, and smokehouse. The Craigs grew buckwheat, rye, oats, flax, hay and corn.

John Jr. and his family were living on the farm during the Revolutionary War Battle of Monmouth on June 28, 1778. In *History of the Old Tennent Church*, Frederick R. Symmes accounted the Craig family's situation on that day:

> There is an interesting tradition connected with the old John Craig farmhouse. . . . John Craig was in the American Army on the day of the battle and left his wife and his one child Amelia and two slaves at the old farmhouse. As soon as Mrs. Craig heard the British were likely to join battle with the American forces near the old farm, she packed her household goods in two wagons and with her child and two slaves rode toward Upper Freehold in the direction from which the British Army had come, thus expecting to avoid molestation. Before leaving the farmhouse she took her silver and placing it in a kettle, sunk it in the open well. . . . A number of British soldiers were buried back of the house. Lord Stirling's artillery was placed on the high piece of ground on the westerly side of the farm, and there is a tradition that two cannon of the British were sunk in the meadow in the retreat from the Battle.

The house, having been vacated by Mrs. Craig, her daughter, and two slaves, was used during the Battle of Monmouth as a makeshift hospital for wounded and dying British soldiers.

Upon John Jr.'s death in 1824, the farm passed to his son Jonathan—who received half the property—and to his daughters Amelia and Mary—who received one-quarter each. Mary died in 1839 and her share, along with Jonathan's share, was deeded to their sister Amelia. At the time, Amelia was married to Peter Bowne. Amelia and Peter had one daughter, Anna Maria, who married Enoch L. Cowart. Anna Maria inherited the farm when her mother died in 1855. In 1898, Anna Maria died and the farm passed to her husband Enoch, who died in 1908 and bequeathed the property to their son, Samuel Craig Cowart.

At the time he inherited the farm, Samuel resided in a home that he had built at 47 Court Street. He remained at this house while renting the Craig farm to tenant farmers. Samuel was an active member of the Freehold community, a member of the National Society of the Sons of the American Revolution, a historian, and a lawyer. A year after he died in 1943, his widow sold the property to Ernest Tark, who owned it until 1965. Unfortunately, in the 21 years that Tark owned the Craig farm, the property deteriorated significantly. By the twentieth century, it was common practice to hire migrant farm workers and Tark was no exception. He used the Craig House as quarters for his migrant workers, who had no appreciation of the historic value of the property. They damaged the house by

DUBOIS GRAVESITE. Tunis Vanderveer and Mary Jane DuBois lost five daughters, ages 15–21, within one year of each other. Their graves are located in the Maplewood Cemetery. From right: Mary Etta (age 15), Jane T. (gravestone illegible), Elizabeth (died September 1870, age 17 years, 10 months), Lydia Conover (died June 1870, age 20 years), and Sarah Matilda (died October 22, 1871, age 21 years).

doing things such as tearing wood paneling and trim to burn as fuel. Fortunately, when the State of New Jersey acquired the property in 1965, it was still recognizable as a historic colonial home. Through the efforts of the local historical group, the Friends of Monmouth Battlefield, the Craig House was restored and has been open to the general public since 1993.

Other early settlers of Freehold were the DuBois family, originally from France. They moved to Germany and then to Holland. By 1663, Louis and Jacque DuBois had immigrated to America. Louis and Jacque were patentees of New Palentine (now New Paltz, New York) and founders of the Dutch Reformed Church in America. One of Louis's sons settled in Salem County, New Jersey. His son, Louis's grandson, was the father of Benjamin, born on March 30, 1739. Benjamin was pastor of the Freehold and Middletown Reformed Churches for 63 years. He married Phoebe Denise and had a son, Tunis, on February 23, 1773. Tunis married Sarah Van Derveer and they had four children. After Sarah died, Tunis married Sarah Smock and they had five children. Three of these—Henry, Benjamin, and Livingston—were residents of Freehold.

Each of Tunis DuBois's sons in Freehold was a farmer. Henry was born on April 4, 1808 in Freehold and married Margaret Conover on April 18, 1832. Benjamin was born on May 10, 1810 and married Helena Wikoff on February 1,

1832. Their home was in what became the new township of Manalapan in 1848. Livingston was born on April 18, 1827 and married Mary T. Hunt on December 6, 1854. Their farm was located on the present-day site of the Monmouth County Library Headquarters on Symmes Road. The DuBois descendants owned hundreds of acres of farmland in the modern-day area of Symmes and Ryan Roads near Route 9 and contributed to the growth of the Freehold community over the centuries.

The Thompson family was also among the early Freehold settlers. Cornelius (1660–1727) and Elizabeth Almy Morris (1680–1726) owned 3,000 acres of farmland on what was originally known as the Passequenctqua Indian Purchase (c. 1690). They built their home, which was known as the Stone House, in 1702. It was located 4 miles southwest of Freehold Village on the Mount Holly road or Burlington Path, present-day Route 537. Before the courthouse was established in Freehold in 1715, the Thompson's home was sometimes used as a courthouse. During the Revolutionary War, it was used as the British headquarters prior to the Battle of Monmouth.

THE STONE HOUSE. Cornelius Thompson built this old stone house between 1700 and 1710 on his farm at Elton in Freehold Township. The home was destroyed by fire in the twentieth century and all that remains is a small graveyard. This photo was taken in March 1906 by Miss Alice Porteus and presented to George C. Beekman by her father, Thomas Porteus. (Courtesy of Monmouth County Historical Association Library and Archives.)

In 1844, Enoch and Achsah Parker Hendrickson purchased the Thompson property. The farm stayed in the Hendrickson family until they sold it to Garret Hartman in 1909. The house survived into the twentieth century, but was destroyed by fire in 1967. At that time, it was owned by a group of five New York doctors and lawyers who had purchased the property for speculation. A small graveyard is all that remains of Thompson's Stone House. The surrounding farmland has fallen victim to bulldozers and has been developed into tract homes that are part of the Freehold Township community.

The Rhea-Applegate House was also built during this early period, in 1745. It is located in Monmouth Battlefield State Park. During the Battle of Monmouth, General George Washington and his officers used the house as a landmark to position the American troops for defensive action. The house was in desperate need of stabilization and restoration by the late twentieth century and by 1995, funding was obtained to perform the necessary work. The exterior was restored, 1.4 miles of eighteenth-century rail fencing was reconstructed, a colonial wood lot was replanted, and hiking trails were extended throughout the battlefield. Future plans to improve the site include removal of encroaching vegetation on cultivated fields, meadows, lanes, and fence. Reproduction fencing will be installed along the original fence lines and a walking trail with wayside exhibits will be added.

In the early eighteenth century, Levi Solomon built a home across from Moore's Inn. According to a period map drawn by Richard Butler, Moore's Inn burned down at the time of the Battle of Monmouth in June 1778. A new structure was built c. 1793 facing the Monmouth–Mount Holly Road.

Solomon's home was owned by Hannah Solomon, Levi's widow, during the American Revolution and was damaged by British troops as they marched through New Jersey on their way to New York. Part of it needed rebuilding after being damaged by fire. The home has since been relocated away from the roadway to make way for a strip mall and is part of a commercial development. Moore's Inn has been renovated and updated over the years. Part of the original tavern can still be viewed from inside the bar area.

One of the best-documented early farmsteads is the Oakley farm, one of the oldest working farms in Monmouth County. It was listed on the National Register of Historic Places on October 4, 1990. The story of the Oakley farm dates to 1686, when the proprietors of East New Jersey sold a tract of land to John Barclay. John, in turn, transferred the property to Robert Barclay that same year. Robert partitioned a 500-acre tract from the original parcel and sold it to John Reid in 1699. In 1701, Reid subdivided his parcel and sold 200 acres to John Bowne, son of Captain John Bowne—one of the original settlers in Monmouth County and one of its 12 patentees in 1665. It is unlikely either Reid or Bowne lived on this land.

John Bowne owned the tract until 1706, when he sold it to Richard Clark. Clark may have been the first owner to actually live on the land, because when he sold the property to George Walker in 1720, the deed mentioned a house situated on 115.43 acres. The farmhouse was probably a 10-foot by 8-foot settler's cabin with a fieldstone foundation. At some time during Walker's ownership, the house was enlarged to a 1.5-story structure approximately 20 feet wide and 25 feet deep with a 5-foot-by-6-foot porch. Walker died in 1748 and his probate inventory (in the Monmouth County Inventory I 1001, dated May 17, 1748) listed "20 head of cattle, 31 head of sheep, 5 horses, 7 swine, 16 geese and 18 other fowl, as well as wheat, rye and Indian corn, and one male Negro slave."

Walker's son Captain George Walker Jr. inherited the farm. In the mid-eighteenth century, he operated a subsistence farm with the help of his family and slaves. They produced meats and grains including pork, beef, poultry, wheat, rye, and Indian corn. Captain Walker served in the Revolutionary War and died intestate in 1794. Aaron Forman Walker was the administrator of the estate and in 1801, sold the 239.9-acre farm to Elijah Combs.

Combs operated the farm from 1801 to 1832. He raised the roof of the house to a full 2 stories, extended the front of the house 5 feet, and enclosed the porch. Like his predecessors, Combs also operated as a subsistence farm with family and slaves. In addition to the products that had been produced by the Walkers, Combs grew buckwheat, corn, potatoes, and apples—for cider and whiskey—and raised bees. His 1831 probate inventory included a house, barn, calf house, corn crib, wagon house, weave shop, unspecified shop, ice house, cow house, sheep house, stile house, cider house, and one lot of beehives.

In 1832, the Commissioners of Monmouth County sold Combs's farmstead, which now consisted of 226.45 acres, to Rulif R. Schenck. Schenck subdivided the land and sold off 83.22 acres before selling the remaining 143.23 acres to Richard S. Hartshorne Jr. in 1842. Hartshorne was was born in Matawan, a descendant of Richard Hartshorne—another Monmouth Patentee. At the time he purchased the Oakley farm, he was working in the oil business in New York. When he purchased the farm in Freehold, he moved his family there and began a commercial farming operation. By the mid-nineteenth century, Hartshorne had introduced gang plows, Thompson's and Biddles' potato diggers, a windmill, a hay tender, a grain drill, mowing machines, and a threshing machine. A silo replaced the corn crib and the farm changed from a subsistence operation to a commercial endeavor. Hartshorne also made some changes to the farmhouse, including the addition of an Italianate porch around 1850.

On April 1, 1871, Hartshorne moved his family into a newer home in Freehold, but continued the farming operation. A little more than a year later, in July, Hartshorne slipped and fell 20 feet from the hayloft in the barn to the floor below. He died from his injuries three weeks later on July 29. A year after Richard's death, his son Acton Civil Hartshorne purchased the property from his father's estate. Acton was a prominent lawyer who lived and worked in Freehold while he leased the farm to tenant farmers. The value of the farm business decreased dramatically during this period and didn't begin to recover until Charles Oakley Jr. purchased the farm in 1911.

Oakley installed interior plumbing and electricity. He also renovated a portion of the house in 1924 to provide housing for his son's family. Under Oakley's

OAKLEY FARM. Charles Oakley Jr. purchased this property in 1911 and made several improvements, including the addition of plumbing and electricity. His daughter Elizabeth was the last owner before the property was purchased by Freehold Township in 1999. (Courtesy of Nancy DuBois Wood.)

ownership, the farm became almost totally mechanized. He raised apples, potatoes, various grains, hay, hogs, chickens, and a milk cow. The farm prospered and when Oakley died in 1932, his daughter Elizabeth continued the operation for 40 years. In 1972, Elizabeth leased the farm for soybean and corn production, and later for sod production.

The farmstead as it exists today consists of a main farmhouse and ten wood frame outbuildings, including a well house, three barns, three sheds, a tenant house (formerly the feed house), garage (formerly the smoke house), wood house, and manure house (converted for residential use). The oldest barn on the property was removed when Route 33 was built and reassembled at Historic Smithville in Atlantic County. There is an 18-acre apple orchard, 82 acres of cultivated field, a 10.2-acre field, and a 2.3-acre pasture. The farm was split by the construction of Route 33: 88.71 acres are to the south of the new road and 26.63 acres are to the north. Freehold Township purchased the property after 1999 and the home has been preserved by the Freehold Township Historical Commission as the Oakley Farmhouse.

An entire book can be dedicated to stories of the countless early settlers in Freehold. Their homes, farms, and businesses contributed to the growth of this area. But there is one individual whose discovery had a profound effect on the economy of Freehold that lasted for more than a century. His name was Peter Schenck.

Schenck was a descendent of one of Freehold's early settler families. In 1768, he made a discovery that had a profound impact on the economy of Freehold for more than a century. Schenck owned a farm in what is now Marlboro Township. He spread soil dug from nearby ditches over his fields and was amazed to find that the crops produced on these fields were of a higher quality than those from fields that were not enhanced by such soil. Schenck identified the soil as marl (glauconite), or green sand, which is the remains of prehistoric fish, clams, and other seafaring creatures from the period in which New Jersey was part of the Atlantic Ocean bed. Marl proved to be a superb natural fertilizer, especially in the production of potatoes, which became Freehold's most precious cash crop. Marl reduces acidity in the soil by providing lime, phosphoric acid, and potassium. The result is superbly fertile farmland.

It didn't take long for local farmers to learn about marl and begin using it on their farms. Word spread about the high quality of the produce that sprang from earth fertilized with marl and demand grew into a prosperous industry, which reached its height between 1860 and 1890. By the mid-1880s, as railroads became an important part of commercial growth in Freehold, the marl industry was comparable to Pennsylvania's coal mining as one of the lucrative businesses of the century. The demand for marl slowly faded away, however, as the new century approached. As new products were introduced during the industrial revolution, the marl industry disappeared.

4. THE CHURCHES OF MONMOUTH COURT HOUSE

The eighteenth century was a period of growth and development throughout the American colonies. In Freehold, families worked hard to make their farmland productive. The town grew into its role as the county seat, and its increased population demanded more churches to tend to religious needs. St. Peter's Episcopal parish was the first congregation established in Monmouth County. It was organized with three branches: one in Shrewsbury, one in Middletown, and one in Freehold. By the 1830s, the three branches became separate congregations serving their individual communities. The history of St. Peter's branch in Freehold began in 1702.

On October 10th of that year, Reverend George Keith presided over the first service for St. Peter's parish at the Quaker Meeting House in Topanemus, owned by Thomas Boels. When Boels died in 1709, he left the meeting house and its grounds with a monetary donation of £6 to the parish. His will, dated March 20, 1710, reads, ". . . all my Right . . . of that acer and a halfe of land and meteing house at Topanemes to ye Espiseapall Church of England as now Estableshed for to bould a Church on also . . . Six pounds toward the boulding of a Church there." The congregation held services in the building and in the homes of parishioners for over 30 years before receiving its official charter.

By 1729, the members of St. Peter's parish had grown to about 500. Between 1729 and 1736, under the guidance of Reverend Forbes, they built a church at Topanemus on Boels's property. When Reverend Forbes died in 1736, Reverend Skinner took over leadership. One of his first moves was to plead with the Society for the Propagation of the Gospel to grant a charter to the congregation and to appoint a missionary leader. Petitioners were John Campbell, William Nichols, Joseph Newton, James Anderson, Joseph Throckmorton, Job Throckmorton, Thomas Hankinson, Matthew Rea, James Day, Kenneth Anderson, and William Madock. The church—represented by John Hamilton, President of Council—received its charter from King George II on June 4, 1736.

Two years later, on August 18, 1738, church leaders purchased a piece of property from James Robinson to build a house of worship. Robert Smith of

Philadelphia was hired to design the church. Smith was also the designer of Carpenter's Hall in Philadelphia and Nassau Hall in Princeton. Construction of the 35-by-52-foot building began in 1771, but due to the interference of the Revolutionary War, was not completed until between 1792 and 1806. The church remains on its original site at 33 Throckmorton Street at the corner of East Main Street. It is the only known eighteenth-century building in Freehold and is listed on the National and State Register of Historic Places.

The church building underwent several interior changes and additions to conform to the High Church ideals of the Oxford Movement. This simply meant that the Episcopal church aligned itself more closely to the sacred rituals of the Catholic Church. The high arched ceiling was replaced with a flat one, the pulpit and communion table were moved to the east side, and the pews were repositioned to face east. Satisfied that the changes conformed to the ideals of the Oxford movement, Right Reverend George W. Doane, Bishop of New Jersey, consecrated the church on May 8, 1838.

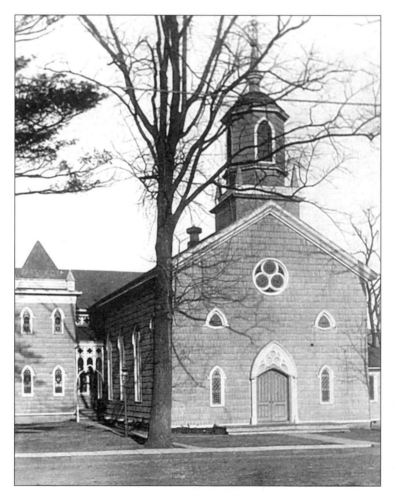

ST. PETER'S EPISCOPAL CHURCH. This is the oldest church in Freehold. Howard E. Thompson was rector when this photo was taken. (Courtesy of Monmouth County Historical Association Library and Archives.)

OLD TENNENT PARSONAGE. The history of the Presbyterian community in Freehold dates back to 1685. This postcard of the parsonage is from sometime in the mid- to late-nineteenth century. (Courtesy of Randall Gabrielan.)

In 1841, St. Peter's was the first church in Monmouth County to receive a pipe organ. In 1855, a chancel (the space where the altar and sometimes a choir are located) was created. In 1859, gas lamps were installed and in 1870 a 408-pound bell was added to the steeple. In 1878, the nave was extended 16 feet to the east, a vestry room was added, and the ceiling was changed back to its original high-arch construction. St. Peter's underwent more renovations, changes, and repairs through the 1890s and again in 1950. Improvements included ten Belgian-made Stations of the Cross in 1935 and a new pipe organ in 1958. As you enter St. Peter's Church today, the original structure is visible from the second pew. As the structure has changed over the years, so have the demographics of Freehold. St. Peter's congregation, through the direction of its rectors, meets the needs of the people of Freehold today. It works with other churches in the area to collect donations and serve meals to the hungry and also runs a charity thrift shop and after-school programs.

The original site of St. Peter's in Topanemus on Thomas Boels's property contained a graveyard. After the church was built in Freehold, there was concern that the gravestones at the original site might be vulnerable to vandals. So in 1970, a group of parish volunteers moved them to the new location. These early gravestones protrude from the earth at the corner of Main and Throckmorton Streets, although the actual graves remain at their original site, surrounded by a modern-day housing development.

Another prominent congregation in Freehold is the Presbyterian, whose history is somewhat complex. The most definitive information available is in two sources.

OLD TENNENT
CHURCH, 1995.
This twentieth-
century photograph
of the Old Tennent
Church shows how
it has weathered
time. (Courtesy of
Nancy DuBois
Wood.)

History of the Old Tennent Church was compiled in 1904 by the church's 50th pastor, Reverend Frank R. Symmes, and covers the story through 1890. *History of Old Tennent Church* by Hamilton Stillwell picks up where Symmes left off and ends in the 1980s. The first Presbyterians to settle in Freehold were from Scotland. In December 1685, 54 Presbyterians from the Campbell clan (who had been persecuted by the Catholic King James II of England) immigrated to East Jersey under the leadership of Lord Neil Campbell. John, James, Archibald, and Ursula Craig were part of this group. That same year, Lord George Scot transported 100 prisoners from Dunottar Castle and over 100 other Presbyterians from Scotland to East Jersey. Only 130 of Lord Scot's group completed the journey. Some of the people from these two groups went to New England and other parts of New Jersey, but most settled in Freehold.

Around 1703, Colonel Lewis Morris sent a letter to the King of England requesting that a missionary be sent to East Jersey to serve its growing Presbyterian community. In the letter, he stated that "Freehold was settled by emigrants from Scotland. Mr. Keith began the first settlement there and made a fine plantation. One-half of the people were Scotch Presbyterians." The other half were Episcopalians, led by Reverend Keith, who had started St. Peter's Episcopal parish in 1702.

It took some time for the Presbyterian congregation to organize. On February 21, 1750, it received a royal charter and the corporate name, "The First Presbyterian Church of the County of Monmouth." Several churches were part of the original charter including Old Tennent Church and Allentown Presbyterian Church (both organized in 1725), Shrewsbury Presbyterian Church (organized in 1734), and Cranbury Presbyterian Church (organized in 1738). The first trustees of the charter were John Little Jr. and Christopher Longstreet of Shrewsbury; Jonathan Forman, Esq.; John Anderson, Esq.; James Robinson and John Henderson of Old Tennent; Robert Imlay and Tobias Polhemus of Allentown; and Stephen Pangburn, Esq. Three church buildings were associated with the Old Tennent Church congregation: Old Scots Church in Marlboro Township; Old Tennent Church in Manalapan; and First Presbyterian Church in Freehold Borough. The Old Scots Church has long since faded into obscurity and its congregation joined the Old Tennent Church. The latter two churches are still standing and home to active congregations.

Two miles north of the Old Quaker Meeting House—site of the original service of St. Peter's Episcopal parish—a crude log structure was built to house the growing Presbyterian congregation. The exact date of the formation of the congregation and the building of its first church is conjecture based on documents such as a letter written in 1792 by John Woodhull, D.D., which states, "the church was formed about an hundred years ago, chiefly by persons from Scotland." Symmes goes on to discuss other probabilities and comes to the conclusion that there is no definitive answer as to exactly when Old Scots Church was organized. Later, it was known as Freehold Church. John Craig Sr. and other members of the congregation applied for registration in 1705. Although the date of the congregation formation is uncertain, it is clear that by 1749 services were no longer held at Old Scots Church. Today, there is no trace of the old log structure that served the religious needs of the original settlers of Freehold. Its location was on the site of what remains today as Old Scots Burial Ground on the northwest side of Wyncrest Road, one-quarter mile north of Route 520 and 6 miles northwest of Freehold Borough. Symmes described the site as "a lonely, retired, and sacred God's acre, in Marlboro Township, Monmouth County, and near to Wickatunk depot, Central Railroad of New Jersey." Anyone who passes the spot today, almost 100 years after Symmes wrote his description, sees that his words are still poignantly true. A part of Freehold's history stands in danger of being obliterated by housing developments.

Unlike Old Scots Church, Old Tennent Church has stood the test of time. Its history dates back to pre-Revolutionary times. As Symmes noted, the "Old Tennent edifice was standing twenty-five years before the Declaration was written." Symmes also noted:

Near the center of the rich agricultural county of Monmouth in New Jersey stands an old church building of colonial style and imposing appearance, attracting the attention of passengers in trains on the nearby Pennsylvania Railroad, and the interest of constant visitors who enter its doors and enroll their names in the register on the church desk and who usually come by carriage on the Freehold-Englishtown road crossing the Manalapan and Pattons Corner road.

Actually, there was a meeting house built on what was called White Hill in April 1734. In 1751, construction of a new church building for the Old Tennent congregation began and was completed in 1753. The building was painted white and remained so until 1832, when Reverend McLean had it painted red. At this point, it became known as "The Old Red Church" and was referred to by that name until it was painted white again in 1835. By 1859, the church became known as Tennent Church, named for William Jr. and John Tennent, two of its most influential ministers.

VILLAGE PRESBYTERIAN CHURCH. This church was built to accommodate the Presbyterian congregation in the village of Freehold. It was dedicated in 1837 and was eventually replaced by a larger structure in 1873. (Courtesy of Monmouth County Historical Association Library and Archives.)

There were many interesting leaders of Old Tennent Church, but four in particular were essential to its history: Walter Ker, Reverend Daniel Veach McLean, William Tennent Jr., and John Tennent. Symmes's history provides detailed information about Walter Ker, considered the "Father of Old Tennent." Ker was loyal to the church of Scotland throughout the Presbyterian Revolution, was banished from Scotland, and immigrated to America in 1685. He was indentured for four years. In 1689 he was given 50 acres in Topanemus from an unidentified granter and an additional 30 acres from Thomas Parr on March 2, 1689. Ker eventually owned land in Matawan and in Freehold near the Old Tennent Church. The epitaph carved into his sandstone grave marker at the Old Scots Cemetery sums up his life:

> Here lies what's Mortal of Walter Ker
> Deceased June 10, 1748 in ye 92 year of his age
> who long with Patience Bore lifes heavy load
> Willing to spend & to be spent for God
> the noble Portrait in a line to paint
> he Breath'd a Father liv'd & Dy'd a saint
> Here sleeps in peace the aged sire's Dust
> Till the glad Trump arouse the sleeping Just.

Daniel Veach McLean was born in Fayette County, Pennsylvania on November 24, 1801. After graduating in 1824 from State University in Ross County, Ohio, he went to study at Princeton Theological Seminary for two years. His first assignment as a preacher was at the First Church of Lebanon in Ohio, where he served for two years. In 1832, he became pastor of Old Tennent Church and served in that capacity until the fall of 1836, when he resigned to serve the congregation of the Village Presbyterian Church of Freehold. On June 10, 1835, the cornerstone for that new church was laid at 57 West Main Street. The church incorporated as an offshoot of Old Tennent Church on April 5, 1836. Its building was dedicated on June 17, 1837. On November 1, 1838, after serving two years as a preacher at the Village Presbyterian Church, Reverend McLean was installed as the first pastor in the newly-constructed church and remained in that position for 12 years.

The congregation in the village of Freehold outgrew the Village Presbyterian Church within 40 years and needed a larger building. Accordingly, a piece of land on the corner of Main and Brinckerhoff Streets was purchased for $4,937.50. The new building's design was in the style of the First Presbyterian Churches in Newton, Sussex County, New Jersey and on Fifth Avenue in New York City. On August 30, 1871, its cornerstone was laid. Brownstone was brought in from Trenton, New Jersey for construction of the building. Faulty stonework led to a lawsuit between carpenters and masons. The final cost of $74,767.21 was more than double the original estimated cost of $35,000. The new church was located at 118 West Main Street in Freehold Borough and had a capacity of 1,000. The

PRESBYTERIAN CHURCH. This postcard shows the latest Presbyterian Church built in the Borough of Freehold. It is postmarked January 3, 1914. (Courtesy of Randall Gabrielan.)

structure included a 190-foot spire, slate roof, gallery, bell tower, and a room in the rear that was used for lectures and Sunday school. Once the building was dedicated on April 10, 1873, its name was changed to First Presbyterian Church.

The congregation was in the new church less than a year, when a severe storm hit in the winter of 1873. The south gable was brought down and it had to be rebuilt. Almost a year later, in September 1874, the new gable was completed and dedicated. Then two years later, some structural instability was found in the bell tower. Fearing for the safety of the congregation, the church council decided to remove it and in 1887, held a fund-raising drive for that purpose. Once again, cost estimates were way off. The original estimate was $2,500, but the final cost turned out to be $10,000. The reason for the disparity was that the spire supporting the bell tower was not substantial enough to hold the new tower. The spire was thus moved from its position in the southwest of the sanctuary to the northwest. Ten years later, the roof over the lecture room was damaged and needed repair.

In February 1891, almost 20 years after the congregation began worshipping in their church, they agreed that it was time to provide a residence for their pastor. The resulting manse served until 1957, when a new one was built. The old rectory was renamed Fellowship Hall and then demolished after 1967. The congregation celebrated the 75th anniversary of the construction of the old Village Church by installing a stone tablet from the old church in the narthex (the lobby to the nave) of the new church. In 1937, the sanctuary needed to be repaired as a result of a fire in the beams behind the organ. A new Baldwin organ was installed in 1950 and replaced by an Austin pipe organ in 1981. Sometime before 1970, the Christian Education Building was added to the site.

The First Presbyterian Church hosted a historical event during a time when ecumenism was a priority throughout the Christian world. The First Union World Wide Communion was held on October 5, 1958. This was a special celebration joining the pastors, choirs, and communion servers from three of Freehold's churches: First Presbyterian Church, First Baptist Church, and Reformed Church. This event was significant because it was the first time that members from three denominations came together to worship.

DUTCH REFORMED CHURCH, c. 1907. This is the edifice of the Dutch Reformed Church in Freehold as it appeared around 1907. (Courtesy of Monmouth County Historical Association Library and Archives.)

METHODIST EPISCOPAL CHURCH. The Methodist Episcopal congregation in Freehold worshipped in temporary quarters for 25 years before they had this permanent home. It was dedicated on April 25, 1858. (Courtesy of Randall Gabrielan.)

In the late seventeenth century, preachers from Kings County, Long Island came to Freehold to serve its Dutch Reformed community. The first preachers were Wilhelmus Lupardus, Vincentius Antonides, and Bernardus Freeman. On October 19, 1709, Reverend Joseph Morgan was installed as pastor of the Congregation of the Navasink—as the Reformed Church was known in the early days—and served until 1731. He occupied a parsonage situated on 100 acres located in Freehold. The congregation was made up of families from both Freehold and Middletown. Those in Middletown worshiped in a church located in an area known today as Holmdel. Those in Freehold worshiped in a church located on Hendrickson's Hill in the area of present-day Hudson Street, Marlboro. In 1731, a larger church was built in Freehold on the current site of the Dutch Reformed Church on Newman Springs Road, east of Route 79. This building served the congregation for 94 years, but in 1826 was razed to accommodate a larger structure. While the new church was constructed, services were held in various locations such as the Monmouth Courthouse, and in homes and barns. The new church was completed within a year—at a cost of more than $10,000—and dedicated on September 9, 1827. In 1931, its name was legally changed from the First Reformed Church of Freehold to the Old Brick Reformed Church.

One of its most influential pastors was Benjamin DuBois, who served from 1764 to 1827. He is noted for having the longest pastorate in the history of the Dutch Reformed Church in America and for introducing English in the church services. Reverend DuBois was also instrumental in the American Revolution, taking part in several raids.

Reverend James Otterman, pastor of the Dutch Reformed Church, purchased two lots in the village of Freehold in 1835 and construction of a new church began. The 1827 building was located on Newman Springs Road east of 79 and served the families of Middletown. The families in Freehold worshipped in the church on Hendrickson's Hill, Marlboro. The lots that Reverend Otterman purchased were in the village of Freehold. The church that was built on this property and dedicated on February 1, 1838 was known as the Village Church.

SITE OF THE ORIGINAL FIRST BAPTIST CHURCH. *This marker is a reminder of the original site of the First Baptist Church, organized in 1834. A new building was constructed in 1846 on West Main Street.*

FREEHOLD BAPTIST CHURCH C. 1889. The church changed its name to First Baptist Church in 1900. (Courtesy of Monmouth County Historical Association Library and Archives.)

The church did not have sufficient funds, so construction was halted for almost two years. Then, John H. Smock advanced enough money to complete the project. On February 1, 1838, the new church was dedicated. Unfortunately, the loan from Smock left the congregation in debt for many years.

There was an attempt to consolidate the Freehold and Middletown congregations, but the people of the Village Church in Freehold did not embrace such an arrangement. In October 1842, they organized as the Second Reformed Church of Freehold. The new congregation made several repairs and improvements over the years. In 1847, a house on East Main Street was purchased for use as the pastor's residence. In 1860, the edifice of the church building was repaired and the church enlarged. The church was refurnished in 1882.

By the 1830s, the Episcopal, Presbyterian, and Dutch Reformed churches were well established in Freehold, but other religious sects also needed places of worship. By 1850, the Methodists and the Baptists built churches in Freehold. The Methodist community began meeting in 1831 at an old store house near Mount's Corner in West Freehold. Reverend James McBurney served as leader. Over the years, meetings were held at the academy on East Main Street in Freehold. Meetings continued to be held in schoolhouses and private homes for two years, until the need to establish a permanent home was imperative. On March 2, 1833, a meeting was held to discuss preparations for building a church. Reverend Thomas G. Stewart, Alfred Hance, Joseph Murphy, Enos R. Bartleson, Ralph Hulse, Samuel Conover, and Jacob Blakesley were elected trustees of the Methodist Episcopal Congregation of the Wesleyan Chapel in the Village of Freehold. Later that month, the trustees swore oaths to uphold the Constitution of the United States, to be faithful to the laws of the State of New Jersey, and to faithfully execute the trust of their office. Within the year, the congregation built a church on West Main Street.

In 1857, Reverend J.B. Graw was installed as the congregation's new leader. It was through his efforts that, on August 25, a cornerstone for a new church building was laid at 91 West Main Street. In less than a year, the structure was completed and after worshipping in temporary quarters for almost 25 years, the Methodist community had a church. On April 25, 1858, the new Methodist Episcopal Church was dedicated. The dedication ceremony yielded donations amounting to $720, enough to offset the cost of building the church. A description of the building was printed in the April 29 *Monmouth Democrat*:

> The new church was designed by Mr. Charles Graham, architect, of Trenton. The style of architecture is called Romanesque. The main building is 40 by 60 feet, with a recess of 5 feet for the pulpit, and a vestibule 8 by 12 feet in the tower, leaving almost the entire main building for the audience room; the tower is finished at the top with a great belfry, and the building is finished outside in imitation of brown stone; the audience room is large and airy, with five long windows on each side, arched at the top; the wood work is grained in imitation of oak, with black walnut trimmings; there is a gallery across the front of the house, but none at the sides, which gives the room a lighter and more pleasant appearance.

Eleven years later, on December 27, 1869, a parsonage was completed. In 1885, the church underwent some remodeling. A tower was added to the front of the building and served as the main entrance. Classrooms and a lecture room were added to the rear of the church. In 1959, an education building was added and named Wesley Hall.

The church, originally known as the Weslyan Chapel in the Village of Freehold, formally changed its name to the Freehold Methodist Episcopal Church on February 19, 1875. Then, in 1968 it united with the Evangelical United Brethren Church and became known as the First United Methodist Church.

The Freehold Baptist Church organized in 1834 from the Upper Freehold Baptist meeting. The congregation built their first church at 81 West Main Street in 1846 and dedicated it the following year. In 1889, they constructed a larger building and added a Sunday school in 1896. In 1900, the church's name was changed from the Freehold Baptist Church to the First Baptist Church.

An African-American community had been established in Freehold as far back as the early nineteenth century, in an area called Squirrel Town. The Bethel African Methodist Episcopal Church was established in 1848 to serve its religious needs. A deed recorded in December 1867 indicates that the owners of the property—Charles C. Browne, his wife Liza Ann, and Joseph Coombs—sold it to the original trustees of the Bethel A.M.E. Church—George Fields, Charles Brindley, Simm Johnson, Theodore Jackson, William Hopkins, and Isaiah Freeman—for $200. The original church was built on this 1-acre lot located off Route 522 (Englishtown Road). It was a small, wood-frame building with a churchyard that was used as a burial ground. Its tombstones tell the story of an African-American community that sent a number of men to the Civil War. One, Charles M. Johnson, was born on July 14, 1827 and died on November 12, 1887. Engraved on his headstone are the words "Colored Troop 22."

The church on Englishtown Road served the congregation for 30 years, until they purchased a piece of land on the corner of Haley Street and Avenue A. Once a new church was built in 1895, the congregation moved its services there and abandoned the old building. In May 1987, a new church was dedicated at 3 Waterworks Road in Freehold Township. Shortly after the dedication, the original church and graveyard were designated a historic site.

BETHEL AFRICAN METHODIST EPISCOPAL CHURCH. This is the second church built for the African-American community in Freehold. It is located on Haley Street and Avenue A. (Courtesy of Rich Walling.)

5. MONMOUTH COURT HOUSE IN THE AMERICAN REVOLUTION

As the American Revolution was taking hold in the newly formed United States, the colonists were divided in their loyalties. Some, the Loyalists (also referred to by the derogatory name Tory), supported the king. Others, the Patriots, favored independence and were willing to fight for it. They were referred to by British supporters as rebels. Others were undecided or changed their loyalties according to who was in town and what the situation was at the time. They might host a meeting of revolutionary Patriot planners in their homes during the day and serve dinner to British or Loyalist soldiers at night. In Monmouth Court House, a large part of the population was Patriot and showed ardent support of the new nation prior to, during, and after the war.

From the 1770s to the 1780s, New Jersey was recognized as the "Crossroads of the American Revolution" because of its position between New York and Philadelphia. Similarly, Monmouth Court House was at the heart of the state of New Jersey. The town functioned as a hub of communication, with taverns serving as essential meeting places. One of the earliest recorded tavern owners in Monmouth Court House was James Wall. There is evidence that Wall was a tavern-keeper as early as 1778, but the location of his establishment is not certain. At times during the Revolutionary War, taverns were used to quarter both American and British soldiers. More importantly, they provided the common colonial traveler with food, drink, and rest, as well as the latest news of revolutionary activities from newspapers, broadsides, pamphlets, or meetings.

During the Revolution, there was only one local newspaper, the *New Jersey Gazette*, published by Isaac Collins. Pamphlets such as Thomas Paine's *The Crisis* were also available. There was no post office in Monmouth Court House, but that did not stop letters from being exchanged. Sometimes, letters were delivered by people stopping at a tavern as they traveled through town. Earlier, in the 1760s, the colonists set up a number of committees of correspondence that exchanged messages between town leaders—often delivered at committee meetings held in a tavern. Taverns also served as meeting places for local residents to come and hear important information from community leaders.

One such meeting took place in June 1774, in response to the events in Boston that had started with the Boston Tea Party on December 16, 1773 and the closing of the Boston port. This quote is taken from Edwin Salter's *History of Monmouth and Ocean Counties, N.J.* His research led him to believe that this was the first meeting of a revolutionary nature in New Jersey:

> The citizens of Freehold [Monmouth Court House] had the honor, we believe, of holding the first meeting in New Jersey to denounce the tyrannical acts of Great Britain—inaugurating the movements in our state which finally resulted in Independence. The date of their first meeting is June 6, 1774; the earliest date of a meeting in any other place that we have met with is of a meeting at Newark, June 11, 1774.

The participants agreed to an embargo on imports and exports from Great Britain and the West Indies. They resolved to create the first local committee of correspondence and allowed the colonists of Monmouth Court House, along with colonists from around the state, to take any measures, such as embargoes, to protect North America from the British during the turbulent times. The committee—comprised of John Anderson, Esq., Hendrick Smock, Asher Holmes, Peter Forman, John Forman, Captain Jonathan Covenhoven, and Dr. Nathaniel Scudder—was also charged with influencing public opinion in favor of independence.

In 1778, George Washington rallied his troops at the Battle of Monmouth. Today, the County offers modern and traditional residential areas, recreation on the Atlantic Coast, and plenty of open land for new office, research and production facilities.

BATTLE OF MONMOUTH. General George Washington leads the charge at the Battle of Monmouth on June 28, 1778. (Courtesy of Randall Gabrielan.)

After the Boston Tea Party, England imposed an embargo on all food items and sundry supplies to Boston. As a result, many colonists were starving and dying. The people of Monmouth Court House responded with necessary supplies and messages of encouragement and promises of more supplies, which they upheld. They also offered to provide necessary supplies to Bostonians. The first shipment included 1,140 bushels of rye and 50 barrels of rye meal. The Bostonians sent a letter dated October 21, 1774, thanking them for their generous contributions. In mid-July 1776, days after the Declaration of Independence was adopted in Philadelphia, residents of Monmouth County gathered on the courthouse steps and listened as Thomas Jefferson's words were read.

The war was in its third year when Monmouth Court House experienced one of its bloodiest battles. The events leading up to the conflict spanned about two weeks, as the British moved from Philadelphia to Sandy Hook. On May 8, 1778, General Henry Clinton replaced General Howe as commander-in-chief of the British Army in Philadelphia. After months of waiting for the right opportunity to strike a final destructive blow to the rebels, Clinton ordered his troops to return to New York, where they would be deployed to the southern states. Fearing a naval blockade of the Delaware River region by the French—who had aligned themselves with the American rebels—Clinton marched across New Jersey, which he decided was the quickest and the most direct route to Sandy Hook on New Jersey's eastern shore. The march was set in motion on June 18th and brought the British army through Haddonfield, Evesham, Mt. Holly, Black Horse, Crosswicks, Allentown, and into Monmouth Court House. As the British and Hessians marched across New Jersey, they were slowed by antagonistic threats from General William Maxwell's New Jersey Continental Brigade, General Philemon Dickinson's New Jersey Militia, and other Patriot groups. On June 28, 1778, the American Continental Army and the British Army met on hilly farmland only miles from the heart of the county seat.

The summer heat was so intense that it is believed to have caused many of the casualties of the Battle of Monmouth. Hundreds of soldiers were taken to the courthouse, Old Tennent Church, the Village Presbyterian Church, and several private homes—which served as temporary medical facilities. Visitors to Old Tennent Church today can see what appear to be bloodstains on some of the pews, purported to be the blood of soldiers from the Battle of Monmouth.

Sunset brought some relief from the heat and both sides broke away from the fighting. Hundreds of dead and wounded were strewn across the battlefield. The injured were carried off to makeshift hospitals and the dead were buried. At the end of the day, 2,400 British soldiers were killed, wounded, captured, or missing. These British casualties included an estimated 1,000 deserters and 40 wounded who were left behind at St. Peter's. The Americans reported 360 casualties and estimated that they buried about 400 British soldiers.

General Washington planned to resume fighting in the morning, but as dawn broke, he discovered the enemy gone. The British had regrouped and silently marched off to the highlands of Lincroft and Middletown. Washington held a

MOLLY PITCHER AT THE BATTLE OF MONMOUTH. The bas relief at the base of the Battle of Monmouth Monument represents Molly taking over at the cannon for her injured husband. The model for the soldier on the left, holding the canon ball, is believed to have been Thomas Edison. (Courtesy of Monmouth County Historical Association Library and Archives.)

council of war and determined that it would be impossible to fight the British at their advantageous perch in the hills. The British made their escape to Sandy Hook and were transported to New York. The Americans moved north to Piscataway, where they celebrated the second anniversary of independence. The Battle of Monmouth proved to the colonists that George Washington was a capable military leader. It also was the first time the Continental Army, newly trained by General Von Steuben, was able to show its worth on the battlefield. Afterward England was left to wonder if it could, in fact, win this war.

Several people from Monmouth Court House who were central to the Revolution are worth mentioning. Nathaniel Scudder was born at Monmouth Court House on May 10, 1733. He was a graduate of Princeton College, studied medicine, and practiced in Monmouth County. His political career included positions on the Committee of Safety, Provincial Congress, General Assembly, and Continental Congress. He was a signer of the Articles of Confederation and an ardent Patriot who wrote articles opposing the tyrannical acts of King George III. He served as a lieutenant colonel of the 1st Regiment of Monmouth in the

New Jersey Militia in 1776 and again in 1781. He was killed on October 17, 1781, while fighting the British at Blacks Point near Shrewsbury. Reverend John Woodhull gave his eulogy and he was buried in the graveyard at Old Tennent Church.

Thomas Henderson was born on August 15, 1743 in Freehold. His life was similar to Scudder's in that he also studied at Princeton and practiced medicine in Freehold. His political career included serving on the Committee of Safety, Surrogate of Monmouth County, Provincial Council, General Assembly, and Chancery. He was vice president of the State Council, acting governor in 1794, a member of the Fourth Congress, and judge of the Court of Common Pleas. As a military officer, Dr. Henderson served as a lieutenant in the New Jersey Militia (1775), second major in Colonel Charles Stewart's Battalion of Minutemen (February 15, 1776), brigade major in the Monmouth County Militia (April 19, 1776), major in Colonel Nathaniel Heard's Battalion (June 14, 1776), and lieutenant colonel and brigadier major at Monmouth.

Prior to the American Revolution, Dr. Henderson had a comfortable home located near what is today the intersection of Routes 537 and 33. As the British marched through Monmouth Court House days before the Battle of Monmouth, they burned Dr. Henderson's home to the ground. Not long afterward, he built a new home on the site. At the time, his funds were low and so the home was quite simple. He called the modest frame building Cincinnati Hall, in honor of the newly-organized Society of Cincinnati. Dr. Henderson was a prominent resident of Monmouth Court House who used most of his money to support the cause of independence. He was known for his humble hospitality and welcomed all regardless of social status. Dr. Thomas Henderson died on December 15, 1824 in his birthplace and is buried at Old Tennent Cemetery. Sadly, Cincinnati Hall was destroyed by fire sometime in the late nineteenth century.

One of the more colorful characters of the American Revolution was Molly Pitcher. Although she was not a resident of Monmouth Court House, she played a role in the Battle of Monmouth. There has been much conjecture as to her true identity and what really happened on that battlefield in June 1778. Folklore says that Molly hailed from Carlisle, Pennsylvania and that her real name was Mary Hays (1754–1832). She traveled from Pennsylvania as a camp follower accompanying her husband, Private William Hays, a cannoneer in Captain Francis Proctor's artillery company. The story is that Molly earned her nickname by carrying pitchers of water to the soldiers as they braved, not only the formidable British Army, but also the overwhelming heat. Private Joseph Plumb Martin wrote one of the first references to her in his work, *Some of the Adventures, Dangers, and Sufferings of a Revolutionary Soldier*, written in 1830. This account of Martin's memories of the war includes:

> One little incident happened during the heat of the cannonade, which I was an eyewitness to, and which I think would be unpardonable not to mention. A woman whose husband belonged to the artillery and who

was then attached to a piece in the engagement, attached with her husband at the piece the whole time. While in the act of reaching a cartridge and having one of her feet as far before the other as she could step, a canon shot from the enemy passed directly between her legs without doing any other damage than carrying away all the lower part of her petticoat.

Some say that General George Washington rewarded Molly for her bravery during the battle. After the war, Mary Hays returned to Carlisle with her husband. When he died, she married John McCauley. Mary outlived John and earned a living doing laundry and other small jobs for neighbors. She applied for and received a state pension in 1822. Mary Hays McCauley died in Carlisle on January 22, 1832.

Another prominent Revolutionary War hero was Captain Joshua Huddy. Huddy was a resident of the village of Colt's Neck of Freehold Township. As a local tavern keeper, he took an active part in the politics and military affairs of Monmouth County. He was a member of the New Jersey Militia, appointed captain in 1776. He served at major battles and skirmishes throughout the colonies, including the Battle of Monmouth. Although a number of documented events prove Huddy's pluck and loyalty to the Patriot cause, he is most remembered for his heinous murder.

Huddy was appointed captain of the Toms River Block House, located in the southern part of Monmouth County that is today known as Ocean County. The block house was erected to protect the salt works along the Toms River. On March 24, 1782, a group of Loyalists sailed down the Jersey coast and up the river, landing under the cover of darkness and attacking the block house. Huddy and his garrison put up a good defense until their ammunition was depleted and they were forced to surrender. Huddy and several others were taken prisoner and brought to New York ,where they were held captive in the Sugar House prison.

William Franklin, bastard son of Benjamin and last royal governor of New Jersey, was at the time president of the Associated Board of Loyalists. He ordered Huddy's execution in retaliation for the death of Philip White. On April 12, 1782, Captain Richard Lippincott led a group of Loyalists who moved the condemned Huddy from New York to Highlands near Sandy Hook, where they built a makeshift gallows out of a barrel and some logs. They had Huddy write a will and immediately upon his signing it, hung him. Several days after his death, Huddy's body was found by a group of local Patriots who brought it to the home of Captain James Greene in Monmouth Court House. A funeral service was held on the steps of the courthouse. Reverend John Woodhull, pastor of the First Presbyterian Church, gave the eulogy and Huddy was buried in the Old Tennent Church. Today, a memorial stone in the Old Tennent graveyard is dedicated to Huddy by the Captain Joshua Huddy Chapter of the Daughters of the American Revolution, but the exact location of his burial is not known.

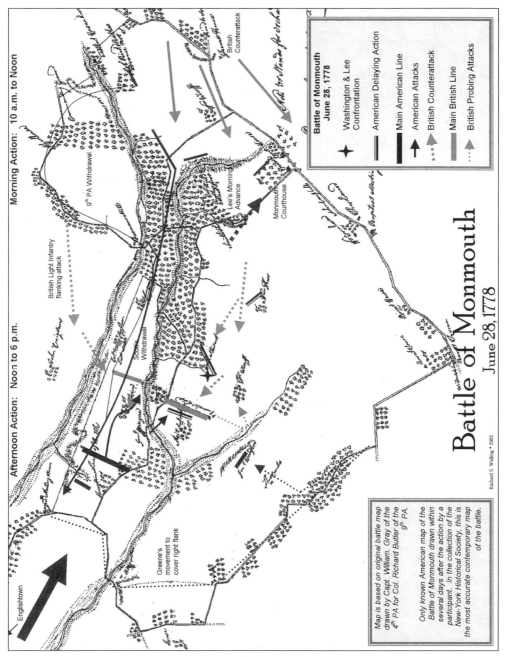

BATTLE OF MONMOUTH MAP. This map is based on an original drawn by Captain William Gray of the 4th Pennsylvania. It shows the movements of the Americans and British as they fought this critical battle on June 28, 1778. (Courtesy of Rich Walling.)

Patriots considered Captain Huddy's death a murder for several reasons. First, the war had ended with the surrender of Cornwallis in Yorktown five months prior to Huddy's capture. Second, the Loyalists cited the death of Philip White as reason for retaliation. In fact, White had been killed after attacking a group of Patriots. Huddy's death was only the beginning of what turned out to be the first international incident for the newly organized United States. The Patriots were irate and petitioned George Washington for satisfaction. Washington asked that Captain Richard Lippencott be handed over and executed in exchange for Huddy, but the British refused. Instead, they court-martialed Lippencott and found him innocent. This only fueled the anger of Monmouth County residents, who continued to pressure Washington to avenge Huddy's death. Finally, Washington asked that a British captain who had been taken prisoner at the surrender in Yorktown be chosen by lottery and executed in exchange for Huddy. The unfortunate captain was Charles Asgill, the son of a very prominent political family in London. Asgill's mother appealed to Count de Vergennes of France to plead for her son's life. He in turn engaged the Dutch and English to intervene. The whole affair cost precious time in the peace negotiations. In the end, Asgill was pardoned and the situation was put to rest.

The Battle of Monmouth and the American Revolution took its toll on the residents of Monmouth Court House in both human casualties and in damage to property, but it did not stop the township from moving forward in a spirit of growth and expansion. As the British moved away from their town towards the Atlantic shore, the residents of Monmouth Court House set about the task of rebuilding and moving forward to be a productive part of the newly-formed United States of America. They rebuilt lost structures, replanted spoiled farms, and reproduced the population—which by 1790, reached an estimated 3,785.

6. THE EVOLUTION OF BUSINESSES AND TOWNSHIPS IN FREEHOLD

The Continental Congress created the American postal system on July 26, 1775 and appointed Benjamin Franklin as postmaster general. By 1800, 51 post offices were in New Jersey. In January 1795, the first post office in Monmouth Court House was established and Samuel M. Kinstry was appointed its first postmaster. When this office was opened, the name of the town was shortened to Monmouth. Three years later, the Township Act of 1798 established the township form of municipal government, but the town did not change its name officially. It continued to be known as Monmouth for three more years, until the post office adopted the name Freehold on January 1, 1801. At that time, Daniel Craig was postmaster. The township has been known as Freehold ever since.

The 1800s were formative years for America. Freehold recuperated from the devastating effects of the Revolutionary War and began shaping its own identity. It was also a time of progress in the commercial arena, as the industrial revolution spurred innovative improvements to production of manufactured and agricultural products. Improvements in agricultural technology helped American farmers produce better and more abundant crops. Increased productivity in mining operations in northwestern New Jersey and in agriculture in southern and central parts of the state were positively affected by the transportation boom between 1800 and 1860. The introduction of the railroad enabled farmers to distribute their produce to a larger market. Freehold farmers were no exception. In fact, Freehold's experience mirrored that of the newly formed United States's political, industrial, and commercial evolution.

During the Revolutionary War, both the Continental and British soldiers had been constantly in search of food and horses—and Freehold's farms provided an ample supply of both. At times, farms were situated along the line of march for battalions. Soldiers showed little mercy in their attempts to get from one place to another: they simply trod over the farmland and, in many cases, destroyed or stole crops, horses, and other livestock. After the war, Freehold farmers had to repair the damage sustained by their farms. As farming was revived, other evidence of development and expansion began to crop up throughout the town. In 1834, Thomas Gordon published an article in his newspaper *Gazetteer*, stating that only about half of Freehold Township's 104,000 acres were being cultivated; the rest of the land was heavily forested with pines. This ratio changed dramatically by the end of the century. Industry and agriculture reached new peaks in production and with these increases came people who needed public services, homes, schools, churches, and places to purchase all the goods that were made available. New businesses opened, more churches were built, and within 50 years of the war's conclusion, Freehold's population nearly doubled to over 6,300 residents.

The taverns that had served as a communication nexus during the war slowly evolved into modern-day hotels. Tavern keepers from the Revolutionary period such as John Anderson, Samuel P. Forman, and Lewis McKnight operated establishments like the Washington Tavern. Tradition has it that this tavern was the "pioneer inn of the village." Its earliest recorded landlord was Major James Craig, sometime between 1797 and 1810. There is speculation that he could have possibly run it before and after that period. Subsequent owners were William Craig, John Caster (in 1818 and again in 1825), Aaron Brewer (1827 to 1830), and

AMERICAN HOTEL. *This is the oldest operating hotel in Freehold and one of a few nineteenth-century establishments still in business today. (Courtesy of Monmouth County Historical Association Library and Archives.)*

General James Ten Eyck. In 1834, Charles C. Higgins bought the Washington Tavern and managed it until 1837. Higgins was a silversmith by trade, but once he tried his hand in the hospitality business, he became one of the most successful tavern keepers in Freehold. After running the Washington Tavern for three years, he went on to own all the hotels in Freehold except the American Hotel. Higgins eventually sold the Washington to Elisha Thompson. Ownership then passed to John J. Thompson, to William D. Oliphant, and to Abner H. Reed. In 1851, David Patterson rented the tavern for one year before he was able to work out a purchase agreement. In 1869, he demolished the house and built a newer, larger building, which he opened as the Washington Hotel in 1873.

Another early tavern was the Union Tavern on South and West Main Streets. The Union was also known as Coward's Tavern, for the first landlord in 1800, Samuel Coward. It was a small, two-story wooden building that was used as the courthouse while a new one was being built *c.* 1806–1808. Its list of proprietors include William Egbert (*c.* 1809), Jacob Dennis (in 1823), and Charles Burk (from 1825 to 1830). Charles C. Higgins ran the Union until he bought the Washington in 1834. Barzillai Hendrickson was next, from 1834 to 1840. Charles C. Higgins returned in 1840 and ran the Union for four years. Nathaniel S. Rue was the landlord from 1844 until 1853. In March 1854, ownership passed to Welch and Carson, who repaired and refitted the house. Carson and Conover ran the new Union between 1856 and 1857. In February 1858, Thomas P. Barkalow purchased the tavern and sold it to Johnson and Patterson in 1866. They ran it until 1869 when Johnson and Bailey became the new owners. It passed to Danser and Sutphin, Richard Fleming, David C. Danser, E.C. Richardson, and finally to John Taylor in 1882. In 1885, 85 years after the Union Tavern opened, its name was changed to Taylor's Hotel. The history of Taylor's Hotel is covered in more depth in a later chapter.

The house adjoining the courthouse on Main Street was owned by John Craig. Between 1830 and 1838, Benjamin Laird ran an establishment there called the Monmouth Hotel. A woman, listed by the name of Mrs. Ware, succeeded Laird as the proprietor and turned it over to hotel tycoon Charles C. Higgins in 1840. Higgins raised the hotel to three stories, totally renovated it, and renamed it the United States Hotel. The United States Hotel had several managers including Benjamin Laird in 1845, John L. Doty from 1846 to 1854, John C. Cox from 1854 to 1855, David C. Conover from 1855 to 1857, and Stokes and Rogers in 1857. Between 1857 and 1864, ownership passed from George H. Snowhill to J.S. Carter to Danser and Hamill, and finally, to David Patterson. Sometime after 1864, Rowland A. Ellis purchased the property and remodeled it into stores and offices, ending the short existence of the United States Hotel in Freehold.

John I. Thompson opened one of America's oldest operating inns around 1834 at 20 East Main Street in Freehold Borough. Thompson operated the hotel under the name Monmouth Hall and owned it until 1837. He then moved to Shrewsbury, but later returned to Freehold and bought the Washington Hotel.

Prior to his death, Thompson sold Monmouth Hall to Isaac Amerman, who ran it until April 1843. David C. Conover bought it from Amerman and ran it until around 1855, when he became the landlord of the United States Hotel. Joseph G. Stillwell was the next owner of Monmouth Hall. He ran it for a few years, then tore it down and built a larger house, which he named the American Hotel.

The American Hotel is one of the few nineteenth century businesses that still exist in Freehold today. Its original operator was J.L. Huntsinger. He was succeeded by John C. Cox, who later went on to run the United States Hotel. Abner H. Reed operated the American from 1854 to 1869 and Mose M. Laird from 1869 to 1873. William Davis was proprietor from 1873 through at least 1875. There were several subsequent owners over the years until 1916, when August Daesner Sr. purchased it. He expanded and upgraded the facility and ran it until his grandson Richard took over the operation. The hotel is still known today as the American Hotel and serves the community as a banquet hall.

The Railroad Hotel was located on Throckmorton Street near the Pennsylvania Railroad station. It opened in 1861 with Charles T. Fleming as its owner. In 1864, William Thompson purchased it and then Thomas Mulholland. The transformation of taverns from small social establishments to larger hotels, along with improved transportation for travelers, made it easier to visit Freehold. This played a major role in the economic growth of Freehold. New businesses cropped up and people moved into the rural area. More buildings were needed for stores, businesses, and homes.

New businesses and residents needed the financial services of a local bank. An early attempt at establishing such an institution was made in 1824. William J. Bowne was manager and cashier of the Monmouth Bank, which opened with $200,000 in capital. The residents of Freehold looked upon the bank with skepticism, though. The bank did not have a safe deposit; ironically, money was stored at the jail. When a safe was finally purchased, the bank carried on its business from Bowne's building on Main Street for about 12 years. On February 23, 1836, the *Monmouth Democrat* printed a notice of sale listing all the bank's assets. It is not certain if this sale ever materialized, because the bank reopened for a short period with Dr. John T. Woodhull as president.

The town of Freehold grew from a central point on Main Street in what is now Freehold Borough. In January 1878, the *Monmouth Democrat* published an account of the layout of the town as recounted by John Richmond Patterson, a 51-year-old resident. Patterson's recollection of the town as it was in 1833 is essentially a list of properties and owners along with some anecdotal information:

> Starting from the Railroad crossing on Main Street, running west, on the south side of the street, the first house was the Dr. John Throckmorton house . . . next came John Outcalt's cabinet ware shop, and then came an old red house...then came the Barkalow house . . . and then the Bruhn house. . . . Then, the old Bowne house. . . . The

MOORE'S TAVERN. This photo shows what Moore's looked like on June 22, 1979. The building was modernized when Route 537 was expanded. (Courtesy of Randall Gabrielan.)

parsonage of the Reformed Dutch church came next, and there was no other house on that side of the street between the Parsonage and the Murphy farm house.

On the north side of Main street, starting with the old Vredenburgh property . . . the old Cottrell property on High street . . . stood back in the fields with a lane leading to it from Main Street. All the land between the church and the railroad crossing, and beyond the church, westerly was farming lands.

Crossing South street, on the corner opposite the court House stood a block of low wooden buildings owned by Judge Vredenburgh. The corner was occupied by William Brown, a gunsmith; next a confectionery and saloon, next the harness factory of White & Reed . . . and next was William I Patterson's tailor shop. . . . Adjoining this block on the east was a small building occupied by Thaddeus Whitlock, a tinsmith. . . . Then came the Washington Hotel . . . then the Elias Hart property . . . then the American Hotel. . . . Next to the hotel was a small store owned by Judge Bruhn, who was also postmaster. . . . Then came the Bennett property . . . then an old red house.

BELMONT HOTEL BEFORE THE FIRE. In 1888, Taylor's Hotel was renovated and renamed the Belmont Hotel. The Belmont is the building on the left. (Courtesy of Freehold Public Library.)

Next to the railroad crossing on the north side of the street stood St. Peter's church. . . . Next came a frame building . . . occupied by the *Inquirer* . . . next the Lippincott property. . . . Next was a dwelling . . . occupied by two ladies named Egbert, who kept a millinery. Then an old building occupied by an Englishman named Vincent, as a confectionery . . . and next an old building occupied by Hon. Daniel B. Ryall as a law office. Next came Mr. Ryall's dwelling then the Throckmorton property . . . and next the old store for many years kept by Co. W.D. Davis.

East of the Court House came the old tavern of Benjamin Laird . . . then the Walter Hart property. . . . Hart was a jeweller and watchmaker, and the first one of that trade in the town. . . . Next came the dwelling of Judge Bruhn; next was John VanCleaf's wheelwright shop. . . . Next was Vancleaf's residence . . . and then came the Academy, where James Shields . . . kept school. The next building was "the Old Tan Yard" property, then owned by Judge Murphy. . . . The next house was below the "elbow" in the road, known as the Bartleson property. . . . Opposite, in the fields, was the residence of Samuel Perrine, a farmer.

This account presents the picture of a central village with businesses and residences lining the main street. As one travels outward from the center of town, acres of farmland were encountered. By the nineteenth century, Freehold's rural setting was transforming into a residential and commercial center. The town bustled with residents and visitors. There were three hotels and stores that sold everything from paper to furniture to groceries to jewelry. Plank sidewalks and dirt or gravel roads were traveled by pedestrians, horse-drawn wagons or carriages, horseback riders, and bicycles. The residential area stood out from the business and commercial activities of Main Street with tree-lined streets. Farmland slowly adapted to commercial endeavors. Today, the town retains its early organization with Main Street as the center of Freehold Borough. The surrounding area, however, is no longer farmland, but instead large housing tracts, the Freehold Raceway Mall, and Monmouth Battlefield.

Freehold residents received their news from the *New Jersey Gazette* until after the War of 1812. The *Gazette* was a Trenton-based newspaper published by Isaac Collins since December 5, 1777. The people of Freehold were also accustomed to reading about special events and urgent news from broadsides. After the War of 1812, John Craig published the *Spirit of Washington* from his home in Freehold.

BELMONT HOTEL AFTER THE FIRE. The February 1933 fire caused over $100,000 in damage to the Belmont Hotel. (Courtesy of Freehold Public Library.)

MONMOUTH DEMOCRAT OFFICE. *The* Monmouth Democrat *was founded in 1834 and served the people of Freehold for almost a century. Pictured in front of the office are Will Ellis and Joseph A. Yard. (Courtesy of Monmouth County Historical Association Library and Archives.)*

This newspaper lasted about one year. Other attempts to establish a newspaper in Freehold were made by West DeKlyn, who began publishing the *Monmouth Star* on October 14, 1819 and the *Monmouth Journal* from December 26, 1826 until 1828. The *Journal* ran into financial difficulties and was barely kept alive by its successor, Major Peter Vanderhoef.

On July 7, 1829, two brothers from Doylestown, Pennsylvania, John Wesley and Enos R. Bartleson, began publishing the *Monmouth Inquirer*. The brothers had heard about the troubled *Journal* and moved quickly to establish a successful periodical in Freehold. In 1860, after several years of struggling and changes in ownership, the current owners, W.D. and J.P. Connolly, consolidated the *Monmouth Star*, *Monmouth Journal*, and *Monmouth Inquirer* and published a new paper under the name *Monmouth Inquirer*. Sometime before 1927, Maxcy Applegate Jr. purchased that *Inquirer*. Upon Applegate's death in 1832, Miss Emma Florence Beach, who had been running the paper since 1927, inherited the paper and sold it to the *Freehold Transcript* on January 27, 1933.

The *Freehold Transcript* had been founded in 1888 by brothers Alex Low and John B. Moreau. Alex and his son Adrien ran the *Transcript* together until Adrien's death from cancer at age 44. Alex's daughter-in-law and Adrien's widow, Anderene Ward Moreau, then took over the paper with the help of her daughters, Leigh and Anderene Natolia. The latter, known as "Tolie," served as editor until she married and moved to north Jersey. After Anderene Ward Moreau died, the *Transcript* was sold to Art S. Schreiber on August 30, 1972. Schreiber was also the publisher of the *Colonial News*, which was published twice a week and mailed to thousands of residents. In January 1974, Schreiber sold the *Freehold Transcript* and the *Colonial News* to the Bergen Evening Record Corporation of Hackensack. Four years later, the two newspapers were merged into the *News Transcript*. In 1981, Greater Media, Inc. bought the *News Transcript* and is still publishing the paper today.

The other major paper that served Freehold was the *Monmouth Democrat*, founded by Bernard Connolly on April 12, 1834. Under Connolly's proprietorship, the paper grew to one of Freehold's most prominent publications. Connolly ran the newspaper for 20 years and then sold it to James Sterling Yard. Yard had learned the art of printing and started Trenton's *Weekly Visitor* in 1846. After just three months, he sold the business. He went on to publish the *Kings County Democrat*, a campaign newspaper based in Williamsburgh, Long Island in 1848. He stayed with the New York paper for two years, then moved back to New Jersey where he printed the first 13 issues of the *Ocean Signal*, which later became Toms River's *Ocean County Courier*. From there, he moved on to Hightstown and started the *Village Record*. Yard had a penchant for starting up newspapers and his next project was the *Long Branch News*, which he created in 1866. This was the last newspaper he published before buying the *Monmouth Democrat* in 1854.

Yard was more than a newspaper publisher. He served as postmaster of Freehold from October 1855 to July 1, 1860. From 1863 until 1865, he served on the Monmouth County Board of Freeholders. During the Civil War, he served as commander of the 28th and 29th Regiments of Volunteers, mustered in Camp Vredenburgh in 1862. Major James Sterling Yard died on April 29, 1900 and is buried next to Governor Joel Parker in Maplewood Cemetery.

In the middle of the nineteenth century, the United States was moving toward Civil War. As the turmoil rose to greater heights, Freehold experienced its own division. Between 1844 and 1869, several villages and hamlets that were part of the original Freehold Township took advantage of the 1798 law that created the township form of municipal government. Before the century was over, several areas split from the township and formed their own independent municipalities.

On February 28, 1844, the New Jersey Legislature passed "an act to set off a new township in the counties of Monmouth and Middlesex, to be called the township of Millstone." The new township was created from parts of Upper Freehold and Freehold in Monmouth County and part of Monroe in Middlesex County. According to the law, the newly-formed municipality was named "The township of Millstone." Its residents held their first annual town meeting at the inn of Ezekiel Davison in the village of Perrineville. Millstone is located southwest of Freehold, in an area of 37.36 square miles bordered by Monroe

BURLINGTON PATH. This is one of the few remaining roads in Freehold that can be traced back to the Burlington Path.

Township in Middlesex County; Manalapan, Freehold, and Upper Freehold in Monmouth County; Jackson in Ocean County; and Roosevelt and East Windsor in Mercer County. Its original boundaries are described with references common in pre-twentieth century land parcel descriptions, such as "in the middle of the Mount Holly road, near Asher Smith's tavern" and "thence up the middle of the said brook easterly, til it strikes the bridge on the land of Joseph I. Ely, son of Isaac Ely, dec'd, in the middle of the new road leading from Hightstown to Britton's tavern, sometimes called the stone tavern." There is a wealth of information in these boundary descriptions, including the identities of people who helped to shape Freehold. For example, in the case of Millstone, we learn that Asher Smith owned a tavern on the Mount Holly road and that Joseph I. Ely's father Isaac was deceased as of the time it was written. We also learn that locals identified Britton's tavern as simply the stone tavern.

On March 6, 1844, just about one week after Millstone was created, another portion of Freehold was set off along with parts of Upper Freehold and Dover Township to form the township of Jackson. At the time it separated from Freehold, Jackson was part of Monmouth County. Six years later, however, Monmouth County was greatly reduced by the creation of Ocean County to its south. Today, Jackson Township is part of Ocean County.

Three years later, on February 18, 1847, the New Jersey Legislature created another new municipality. This new township, named Atlantic, was the result of partitioning parts of Shrewsbury, Freehold and Middletown—the three original townships in Monmouth County. Starting in the southwestern part of Shrewsbury, the new town ran past Jacob Conover's farm, Hulse's house, and John J. Ely's mills, and traversed several brooks. It covered 31.7 square miles. At the time that the township was created, Colt's Neck was designated as a village within Atlantic. Its first town meeting was held at Samuel Laird's hotel. Although the area was called Colt's Neck since colonial times, it was not until 1962 that a referendum officially changed the name from the township of Atlantic to Colt's Neck.

Two more splits came a year after Atlantic was formed. These two new municipalities were derived solely from Freehold Township, one from the north and one from west. The township of Marlborough, established on February 17, 1848, was carved out of the northwestern corner of Freehold. Today, it is surrounded by Freehold to the south, Manalapan to the southwest, Middlesex County to the northwest, Holmdel to the northeast, and Colt's Neck to the southeast. At some point, the spelling of Marlborough was changed to Marlboro. The State Legislature passed another act on March 9, 1848, creating the township of Manalopan, as it is spelled in the book of Public Laws. Today, the township is known as Manalapan. It is bordered by Freehold in the east, Millstone in the south, Middlesex County in the west, and Marlboro in the north. This 32.1-square-mile tract of land is perhaps best remembered for being the site of the Battle of Monmouth, which took place almost 70 years before it was designated as a separate township.

Twenty years elapsed before the next municipal change in Freehold in 1868. At that time, there was a flurry of transportation-related activity as railroad companies organized and tracks were laid in and around Freehold. The county was subdivided and a new county named Ocean, was born on February 15, 1850. When the Civil War was over, the country entered a period of reconstruction and another section of Freehold incorporated as a separate township.

The boundaries of the Town of Freehold were set forth on March 25, 1869 by an act of legislation entitled, "An Act for the improvement of the Town of Freehold, in the County of Monmouth." The area, according to the boundary description, was actually a very small portion of Freehold located in the heart of the township. It was roughly the same area that is today designated as Historic Freehold Center. The legislation provided for the election of a board of commissioners for the Town of Freehold. The Town of Freehold does not exist as such today. It has been absorbed into Freehold Borough. And so the municipal changes came to a halt. The boundaries and political structure of Freehold Township remained the same until the twentieth century.

7. Schools, Railroads, and a Raceway

The populations of Freehold and the newly formed municipalities of the nineteenth century continued to grow. Up until the nineteenth century, children were educated mostly in private homes, churches, or one-room schoolhouses by itinerant teachers. As advancements in agricultural and manufacturing production lessened the need for children to help on the farm, parents began to desire a more formal education. There were no state funds allocated for education until 1829, when the legislature passed an act establishing common schools, including several schools in Freehold.

Several early schools provided education for the children of Freehold. Joseph Rue opened the Latin Grammar School in 1778 and used the home of Henry Perrine for a classroom. The English and Classical School was founded in 1780 on Main Street. The Georgia School House opened in 1795 and Reverend John Woodhull established the Old Tennent Church School in 1799. By the nineteenth century, several more schools existed: the Old Log School House, also known as the Ancient Baptist School (1820); the Paradise School, located on Elton-Adelphia and Jackson Mills Roads (1825); the Select and Classical School (1828); and the Dutch Lane School, also known as East Freehold School, on East Freehold and Dutch Lane Roads (1843). Later, this last school was used as the municipal building.

The Freehold Academy was originally organized in 1831. On August 2, 1836, its trustees bought property adjacent to the existing building on East Main and Spring Streets. This larger plot of land accommodated a larger school that provided excellent education to many young men through the early nineteenth century. In 1844, William W. and Charles F. Woodhull—who had taught at the Freehold Academy—opened the Woodhull School, also known as Monmouth School or Woodhull Institute, at 63 West Main Street. In the 1850s, the Woodhulls moved their preparatory school for boys to the northeast corner of Broad Street and Manalapan Avenue, where it remained in operation until 1874.

In September 1844, Reverend Daniel V. McLean, pastor of the Village Presbyterian Church; Judge Thomas G. Haight; and John Hull organized the

Freehold Young Ladies' Seminary. At a cost of about $10,000, two buildings were erected through the block from Main Street to High Street. The Christian-based curriculum included French, Greek, Latin, chemistry, geology, botany, geometry, music, and drawing. Its first session began on May 17, 1845 and accommodated seven girls brought to Freehold from New England by principal Amos Richardson and his wife. The cost of tuition and boarding was less than $200 per year. The young women who attended the Seminary came from all over the United States, including places like New Marlborough, Massachusetts; Knoxville, Tennessee; and Towonda, Pennsylvania. The school graduated 900 students in its first 25 years. Richardson purchased the school from its founders and served as principal for 36 years, despite an accident that left him blind. In that time, he expanded the school with an additional building on High Street (present-day Broad Street). His daughter Laura Richardson Conover graduated from the Seminary and returned to join the staff as a piano and organ teacher. His son Charles also joined the staff. On October 16, 1881, Richardson died and within two years the Seminary was sold to settle his estate.

A group of prominent Freehold citizens, led by Reverend Frank Chandler, pastor of the Presbyterian Church, and including the Honorable Joel Parker (former governor of New Jersey from 1863 to 1866), formed an association and took on the school's cause to prevent its permanent closure. An advertisement in the September 27, 1883 *Monmouth Democrat* broadcast the opening of the improved Seminary:

FREEHOLD YOUNG LADIES' SEMINARY DWELLING HOUSE. Some students boarded at the seminary. Those who did lived in this building. (Courtesy of Freehold Public Library.)

FREEHOLD YOUNG LADIES' SEMINARY, SEMINARY HALL. This is where most of the classrooms were. (Courtesy of Freehold Public Library.)

THE YOUNG LADIES' SEMINARY

at

FREEHOLD, N.J.

will begin its 40th year

WEDNESDAY, SEPTEMBER 19, 1883

The subscriber, having accepted the presidency of this institution, guarantees to his friends and the public, thorough teaching in the common and highest English branches, in Art and Music, in Ancient and Modern Languages.

Young ladies will be prepared for College, or fitted to grace any social station for which their talents qualify them, and where noble christian womanhood is revered.

The buildings are being put in thorough repair and supplied with modern conveniences, and will be newly furnished throughout by influential and literally minded citizens who have purchased the property.

Our pledge is given to those entering the family that there will be a generous table and a bright christian home, under gentle and restraining religious influence which will be non-sectarian.

The best of teachers are engaged, and it is the purpose of the owners of the property and of all concerned in management, that the institution shall be in no respect second to any of its class in the State or in the country.

For terms and circulars apply to

Rev. FRANK CHANDLER, D.D., Pres.

The association completed major repairs and improvements to the furnishings of the school. They hired two sisters, Eunice D. and Ada Sewell from Portland, Maine, to teach at the school. Eunice served as principal for 12 years and Ada taught literature. When the school year started in September 1883, 40 students were enrolled. After Eunice Sewell resigned as principal, a Mr. Stocking and his daughter ran the school for a short time, although unsuccessfully. In 1897, 53 years after the Freehold Young Ladies Seminary opened its doors, its last commencement was held.

SEMINARY HOUSE ON MAIN STREET. This photo was taken c. 1886. (Courtesy of Monmouth County Historical Association Library and Archives.)

FREEHOLD YOUNG LADIES' SEMINARY. An inscription reads: "From left to right, 1. Floss Layton, 2. Ettie Underhill, 3. Bess Smith, 4. Ted Newton, 5. Marguerite Lowe, 6. Grace Cook. Ada Smith in background playing tennis, covered walk at side." (Courtesy of Monmouth County Historical Association Library and Archives.)

Three years later, in 1900, Colonel Charles J. Wright purchased the buildings that housed the Freehold Young Ladies Seminary along with the adjacent property that was the site of the Freehold Institute. Wright planned to open both these properties once again as educational facilities. The group of buildings that housed the Freehold Institute became the New Jersey Military Academy, which advertised in 1906 that its curriculum focused on preparing young boys for college or business. The annual tuition was $400. Wright reopened the defunct Freehold Young Ladies Seminary as Freehold Military School. He publicized the school, for young boys between the ages of nine and sixteen, with words that would seduce any caring parents into sending their child: "Freehold Military School is designed to meet the needs of a military school for young boys only—an institution where the boy of tender years can benefit by the unquestioned advantages of a military training and be free from the influence of boys of maturer years." While the school's name indicated that it provided military training, the focus was on discipline to prepare the young boys for college. Wright made it clear that this was not a reform school. It was, instead, a place where young boys could be educated in a military style that would develop them into sound, healthy, moral

FREEHOLD MILITARY SCHOOL. In 1900, Colonel Charles J. Wright purchased the Freehold Young Ladies Seminary and reopened it as the Freehold Military Academy. (Courtesy of Monmouth County Historical Association Library and Archives.)

and intelligent candidates for college. Students received personal attention in 40 small classes and a gymnasium allowed participation in all sports. All these scholastic amenities were provided in an atmosphere that, according to Wright, mirrored home. The annual tuition was from $450 to $500.

After Colonel Wright's death, his widow sold the New Jersey Military Academy property to Major Charles M. Duncan, who had been hired to run the Freehold Military School. Duncan kept both schools open under one name, Freehold Military School, until 1916, when he moved the school to a site on South Street. Freehold Borough subsequently took over the Seminary buildings and demolished them. In 1927–1928, the town built a new school, the Broad Street Primary School, which is still used today.

The West Freehold Seminary and Collegiate Institute opened its doors in 1847. The school was situated on a 1-acre lot conveyed to the school's trustees—Samuel Conover, John H. Mount, and William N. Thompson—by Rulif R. Schanck for $25 in 1832. The lot was part of the Oakley farmstead. The one-room schoolhouse was 25 by 40 feet and had hand-hewn beams, sash windows, and a polished wood floor. Six to eight grades were taught. In 1883, the front of the schoolhouse was expanded. In 1911, the school created a larger playground from an adjoining plot of land sold by James Boud to the trustees. Almost 100 years later, a new school was built, known as the West Freehold School. Located on

West Main Street, it opened on September 8, 1936. There were eight classrooms to serve 308 students. This second school has gone through four building additions since then. Today, there are 35 faculty and staff who teach over 240 students from kindergarten through fifth grade. In the early 1990s, the Freehold Township Historic Preservation Commission started a restoration project on the original one-room schoolhouse located on Wemrock Road.

In 1847, Samuel C. Hicks and Oliver R. Willis bought an oat field and built the Freehold Military Institute for Boys the following year. It opened with 11 boarders and 13 day students. By the end of 1849, enrollment had more than doubled to 42 boarders and 10 day students. The September 22, 1859 *Monmouth Democrat* described the campus, located on the northwest corner of South Street and Institute Street (now Lincoln Place):

> The buildings were planned and erected expressly for the purposes of a first class boarding school. The dormitories are spacious having high ceilings, and ventilating flues. The sitting rooms for the boys are warmed by steam, and lighted by gas. The main schoolroom is a fine saloon containing an area of about 200 square yards and has a ceiling 18 feet high. In this room each student is furnished with a neat desk and comfortable chair. The classrooms are large, well ventilated, and furnished with maps, blackboards, globes, etc., for conducting recitations in the most perfect manner. The school and classrooms are

NEW JERSEY MILITARY ACADEMY. One of the amenities of the New Jersey Military Academy was the athletic field, which provided a learning experience for its students in all sports. (Courtesy of Freehold Public Library.)

warmed by both steam and hot air, which combined constitute the most pleasant and healthful mode of warming. The philosophical and chemical apparatus is abundant in supply, and of a superior style of workmanship.

The property on the southeast corner of Georgia and Jackson Mills Roads was originally deeded to Freehold Township by the board of proprietors of East Jersey with the stipulation that it be used for educational purposes in perpetuity. The first school, a log building, was replaced by the Georgia Road School in 1862. This new wooden structure was built just north of the original site and provided education for children from the southeast section of Freehold Township. The school remained open until 1935. It is distinguished as being the first historic property acquired by the township and is in the process of being renovated.

The schools established in the nineteenth century served the Freehold community well. However, as the education system in the United States evolved into a system of elementary, middle, and high schools, Freehold realized the need for the same. Accordingly, in the spring of 1908, the Board of Chosen Freeholders voted to build a new high school on Hudson and Bennett Streets. The construction contract was awarded to H.H. Moore of Spring Lake at a cost of $19,550. The colonial-style red brick building with light gray trim and a slate roof fronted Hudson Street and measured 70 feet wide and 57 feet deep. It housed a gymnasium, training room, lockers, toilets, and heating and ventilating systems in

Georgia Road School, 2002. One of the early schools of Freehold Township, it is slated for restoration.

FREEHOLD HIGH SCHOOL. Built in 1908, Freehold High School was located on Hudson and Bennet Streets. By 1926, it was used as a middle school and today it houses the Freehold Police Department. (Courtesy of Randall Gabrielan.)

the basement. It also contained a library, auditorium, and lecture hall in addition to regular classrooms and the principal's office. The building was fireproof and was equipped with plumbing, electricity, gas, and a telephone system. The school opened with eight teachers. The building housed Freehold High School until 1926, when the Freehold Board of Education (whose members included Alex Low Moreau, founder of the *Freehold Transcript,* and Joseph Brakeley, owner of Brakeley's Canning Company) constructed a newer structure on Broadway (Route 79). The old building at Hudson and Bennett Streets was then used as a middle school and now houses the Freehold Police Department Headquarters.

On October 6, 1953, a referendum was approved organizing seven districts into the Freehold Regional High School District. One of its first actions was to approve an addition to the existing high school. Reflecting the growing enthusiasm for sports, an athletic field was included. Eventually, the high school was purchased from the Freehold Board of Education and in 1955, its name was changed to Freehold Regional High School. Today, the district serves Freehold Township and Freehold Borough, as well as Colts Neck, Howell, Marlboro and Manalapan.

The St. Rose of Lima parish recognized the need for a parochial school and in 1875, constructed one on Orchard Street. In 1911, the school moved to McLean

ST. ROSE OF LIMA PAROCHIAL SCHOOL. Organized in 1875, the Catholic School is run by the Sisters of St. Francis of Philadelphia. (Courtesy of Monmouth County Historical Association Library and Archives.)

Street and in 1957, to Lincoln Street. In 1966, an addition was built on South Street. The Sisters of St. Francis of Philadelphia have run the school since 1878. The history of the parish of St. Rose of Lima dates back more than 20 years before the establishment of the Orchard Street School. Father John Scollard traveled regularly to Freehold to celebrate Catholic mass. On November 10, 1851, he purchased a piece of land to build a frame church to serve the people of the parish.

Since its inception, five pastors have served the parish. Father Alfred Young, from 1857 to 1860, was responsible for purchasing a plot of land to be used as a cemetery. The first resident pastor, Monsignor Frederick Kivelitz, was appointed on January 9, 1871. By this time, the parish was scattered over 125 square miles. In March 1881, Henry A. Young, an architect from Keyport, was hired to design and construct a church on McLean Street. Construction began in the summer of 1881 and was completed by August 1882. An addition was completed in 1921. In 1930, Monsignor John A. Kucker began his service as pastor. Within a year, in October 1931, a rectory was built. Father Thomas P. Ridge succeeded Monsignor Kucker in 1964. He, in turn, was succeeded by Monsignor Thomas A. Coffey in 1971. The parish expanded and a larger church building was constructed in 1980. This new church, known as St. Rose of Lima Chapel, was blessed by Bishop John C. Reiss and had a capacity of 750 people. In 1990, Father Gerard McCarron became its pastor.

In the middle of the nineteenth century, Freehold was a town booming with progress and hope for successful expansion. The *Monmouth Democrat* printed many editorials representative of this spirit. One, published on August 7, 1856, speaks of the building boom of the mid-1850s and mentions several "ornamental and tasty" residences and office buildings:

> What we wish more particularly just now is to call attention of those who are seeking for a good location for a country residence, or to escape from the foul atmosphere and crazy din of the cities, to our beautiful village. In addition to the pure air of the county, we have the advantage of three excellent seminaries of learning, not surpassed in any respect by the best in our land; churches of six denominations of christians; and a railroad conveyance twice a day to the cities of New York and Philadelphia. If any other town in New Jersey can boast of more advantages than Freehold, we should like to know where it is to be found.

By mid-century, Freehold had become a desirable place in which to live and its residents were proud of their community. Perhaps the institution that spurred the most pride was the well-known landmark, Freehold Raceway. Located on Route 9 near the intersection of Routes 33 and 537, the raceway is actually situated in both the Township and the Borough. Horses were an integral part of the Freehold community and horseracing in Freehold dates back at least to the 1830s, when farmers brought their fastest horses to a makeshift racetrack at the same location as today's Freehold Raceway. Country fairs, horseracing meets, and other outdoor events were held at the site for years before the raceway was constructed. One such was an agricultural fair, which some consider to be the beginning of the plans for Freehold Raceway.

On December 17, 1853, a group of Monmouth County residents met at the home of Nathaniel S. Rue near the intersection of Throckmorton and Broad Streets to discuss the possibility of holding an agricultural fair in Monmouth, similar to the yearly fair in Jamesburg. The group established the Monmouth County Agricultural Society and set about making plans for the fair. They elected William Henry Hendrickson as president. James S. Lawrence, Thomas Baird, and John M. Perrine were chosen as vice presidents. John S. Denise, Andrew Simpson, Abram Osborne, John W. Ely, Samuel W. Jones, Pierson Hendrickson, Benjamin W. Corlies, Robert Allen, Peter Smock, Benjamin F. Randolph, and Joseph Combs served as secretaries and Henry Bennett was appointed the treasurer. A lifetime membership cost $10 with an additional annual fee of $1.

From its beginning, the Monmouth County Agricultural Society hosted an annual fair in Freehold Township that included harness racing. The first such fair was in 1854. The society rented a 10-acre piece of land from Hudson Bennett that is part of the present-day site of Freehold Raceway. The rent in 1854 was $50 per year. Four years later, the Society purchased a 20-acre tract of land—including the original 10 rented acres—for the sum of $3,000 from Colonel W.D. Davis. The property was improved in 1875 at a cost of $983.70. As the sport of harness racing gained popularity, the society decided to add a half-mile track and grandstand in 1877 at a cost of $1,650. The raceway flourished until 1888, when the Monmouth County Agricultural Society faced financial problems that eventually led to its demise. The 20-acre property passed into the ownership of James S. Parker, a real estate investor. For eight years he let it fall to ruin.

Sadly, Freehold Raceway ceased to provide the arena for this much-loved sport. But this was only a temporary setback and harness racing was not completely destroyed in Freehold. There was still an interest in the sport and in December 1895, a group of 52 local men organized the Freehold Driving Club. The club negotiated a lease for Freehold Raceway at the rate of $174 per year. On May 19, 1896, the horses were ready for their first race in seven years. Once again, harness racing provided an exciting leisure activity for fans from all over New Jersey. The success of harness racing motivated the Freehold Driving Club to add another dimension to Freehold Raceway.

In 1902, the Freehold Driving Club incorporated, purchased the raceway for $4,500, and built a golf course on the grounds. The harness racing and golf operations were a huge success, but short-lived. While the Freehold Driving Club

FREEHOLD DRIVING ASSOCIATION HORSEMEN'S DINNER, MARCH 31, 1937. The American Hotel hosted the dinner, compliments of Harry S. Gould Sr., who had just purchased Freehold Raceway. (Courtesy of Monmouth County Historical Association Library and Archives.)

VICTORY WHOOP FOR HARNESS RACING'S FIRST MILLIONAIRE. Stanley Dancer (left) lets out a happy yell as Cardigan Bay reaches the finish line in the Freehold Special a length-and-one-quarter ahead of his closest rival. The New Zealand–bred horse became the first in harness racing history to amass $1 million in earnings. (Courtesy of Kat Veneziano.)

was a tenant (1895–1902), it had not been in a position to maintain or to improve the grounds, even when it needed it after seven years of horseracing and golfing. In 1909, unable to do anything about the condition of the raceway, the Driving Club disbanded and a new organization was formed. The Freehold Driving Association incorporated and went about rebuilding the track. Freehold Raceway continued to host the annual fair and occasional races as the popularity of the sport ebbed and waned throughout the next decade. For example, in July 1917, a five-day horseracing event was held with over $1,000 in prizes and the sport once again gained momentum as a major leisure-time activity in Monmouth County. Conversely, a ruling that outlawed racing led to a downward trend in interest by 1921. A slight increase was experienced after Joseph Donahay purchased Freehold Raceway for $10,000 in 1921 and rebuilt the grandstand in 1923, but that interest was short-lived.

Almost ten years later, on September 15, 1936, the newly-organized Freehold Trotting Association reopened a renovated and improved track on the site. Harry S. Gould, an avid sportsman and manufacturer of woven labels from Park Ridge, New Jersey, purchased a share in the track. Then in 1941, Freehold Raceway became the first pari-mutuel track in New Jersey and the first pari-mutuel harness track in the nation. Gould, who was opposed to gambling, consequently sold his share of the track for the sum of $65,000 to Fred Fatzler. Fatzler went to work

FREEHOLD RACEWAY FIRE, MAY 4, 1984. Fire engulfed the grandstand at Freehold Raceway after racing had concluded for the day, so no humans or horses were injured in the blaze. (Courtesy of Carl Beams.)

completing the improvements needed to create the pari-mutuel track—including 24 betting booths, 15 cashier cages, and an infield tote board—at a total cost of $35,000. He operated the track until racing was halted in 1943 due to World War II. The horseracing moratorium lasted only about a year and on July 22, 1944, the Freehold Trotting Association reopened the track.

September 12, 1946 was the start of a 24-day pari-mutuel meeting at Freehold Raceway. The crowd of 4,000 fans was the largest recorded attendance to date. There were ten races and wagering on the first day hit an all time high of over $78,000. Over the course of the meet, more than $1.4 million was wagered. Horseracing in Freehold was here to stay and grew in popularity over a 14-year period, as the number of racing days in each season slowly increased and records were set and broken. Triple Crown and Horse of the Year winners included Albatross, Niatross, Bret Hanover, Cam Fella, Adios Butler, and Keystone Ore. One of the most exciting records was set on October 3, 1953. On that day, three horses—Patchover (#4), Penny Maid (#5), and Payne Hall (#7)—hit the finish line simultaneously, producing the first triple dead heat in harness racing history.

Since the end of World War II, Freehold Raceway has been owned and operated by several different entities. In 1960, Fred Fatzler sold the raceway to Harold and Bernard Sampson of Milwaukee for $5 million—more than $4.5 million more than the price Fatzler had paid almost 20 years earlier. In 1965, Gibraltar Pari-Mutuel of Canada purchased the Raceway from the Sampsons for $8 million. In

1967, Gibraltar Pari-Mutuel reconstructed the starting gate to accommodate eight horses instead of six with two trailers. Shortly after, another record was set. On September 14, 1968 at the Freehold Special, world-renowned Harness Racing Hall of Fame driver Stanley Dancer drove Cardigan Bay to the finish line to win by a length-and-one-quarter. As a result, Cardigan Bay became the first harness horse to win over $1 million in career earnings. Today, Cardigan Bay is honored with an access road named for him at the Freehold Raceway Mall.

Gibraltar Pari-Mutuel continued making significant improvements to the raceway. In 1970, they completed a new enclosed grandstand that could offer year-round horseracing, rain or shine. The sport of harness racing flourished in Freehold and Freehold Raceway became a signature institution in the community. Fourteen years after it had been rebuilt, on May 4, 1984, an all-consuming fire caused by an electrical short completely destroyed the grandstand. Fortunately, the fire broke out after racing had concluded for the day and no spectators nor animals were hurt. However, horseracing was halted for two months until July, when tents were constructed to serve as a makeshift grandstand and pari-mutuel windows were set up outside. The atmosphere was that of a "country fair meet" as the horses and drivers raced around the track. During the winter months, simulcasting was conducted inside "bubbles" similar to those used for indoor tennis. The 1984 harness racing season was saved.

The raceway changed hands again shortly after the fire, on December 31, 1984. The Wilmot family of Rochester, New York purchased the 90-acre track. Their

MOLLY PITCHER RACE, AUGUST 18, 1984. At the half-mile pole, Bunny's Wish (#4) was in the lead. (Courtesy of Freehold Raceway Collection.)

real estate development company, Wilmorite, Inc., began rebuilding a new grandstand and dining room on July 15, 1985 at a cost of over $12 million. Racing continued during the construction and spectators were able to enjoy live horseracing and simulcasting from Meadowlands through January 8, 1986. The renovations and reconstruction project were completed by the fall of 1986 and a gala affair was held on October 22, 1986 to celebrate the opening of the new and improved Freehold Raceway.

The next transition was when the Wilmots decided to change the stabling operation of the raceway. Instead of providing long-term stables, they substituted holding stables. This made approximately 50 acres available behind the raceway. The Wilmots subdivided that parcel and began construction on Freehold Raceway Mall. The mall was designed with its entire motif dedicated to harness racing. It opened its doors on August 1, 1990 and remains a vital part of the commercial activity of Freehold.

OLD-TIMER WINS AGAIN. George McCandless poses with Kehms Scooter after winning on October 21, 1994. The 82-year-old McCandless was the oldest driver to win at Freehold Raceway. (Courtesy of Freehold Raceway Collection.)

MOLLY PITCHER WINNER. Michell's Jackpot (#4) wins the 9th race at the 15th Annual Molly Pitcher 2-Year-Old Filly Pace on September 7, 1996. (Courtesy of Freehold Raceway Collection.)

On September 25, 1990, Kenneth R. Fischer, a retired coffee company executive and owner of the Gaitway Farm in Englishtown, New Jersey, purchased the raceway's operating corporations—Freehold Raceway Association, Atlantic City Harness, Inc., and CIRCA 1850, Inc.—from the Wilmots. During Fischer's ownership, another harness racing record was set. On October 21, 1994, George McCandless—an 82-year-old resident of Vineland, New Jersey—drove Kchms Scooter to victory, making him the oldest driver to win a race in the long history of Freehold Raceway. On February 2, 1995, Fischer sold the racetrack operating companies for $23 million to International Thoroughbred Breeders, Inc. of Cherry Hill, New Jersey—owned by Robert Brennan, noted financier and horseman. Brennan is widely known in the industry for rebuilding Garden State Park in Cherry Hill. The latest change of ownership occurred on January 29, 1999. In four years, the property doubled in value and was purchased by Pennwood Racing for a sum of $46 million.

Besides George McCandless, Freehold Raceway has hosted many other drivers. Hall-of-Famers Stanley Dancer and Bob Farrington both launched their careers there. Another Hall-of-Famer, Herve Filion, set numerous records there. The latest Hall of Fame winner is Freehold resident Catello Manzi. His father Al and uncle John made their careers in harness racing, so Catello grew up around

THE HOME STRETCH. *Frank's Delight stretches for a win in the 8th race at Freehold Raceway on February 2, 1997. (Courtesy of Freehold Raceway Collection.)*

horses. He, however, was drawn to the idea of being a teacher and pursued that career. By 1968, his love of horses lured him away from education. By 1996, Manzi had amassed 7,000 wins at his hometown venue. He also won 14 track championships by 2001. That year, Manzi celebrated 9,000 career wins (ranking him third all-time) and over $82 million in purse earnings (ranking him sixth all-time). In 2002, he was inducted into the Harness Racing Hall of Fame in Goshen, New York.

Harness racing records are not all for winners. On March 18, 2001 a thoroughbred horse named Zippy Chippy won his first race by beating a harness horse nicknamed "Paddy's Laddy." Unfortunately, the race was an exhibition, so Zippy Chippy maintained his record of 89 starts without a victory.

Today, Freehold Raceway's half-mile track stands as a beloved icon. It is the nation's oldest pari-mutuel harness racing track and provides ten months of excitement from August through May. It hosts live standard-bred harness races for trotters and pacers. Some of its more popular races are the Battle of Freehold and the Molly Pitcher Stakes, named for Freehold's Revolutionary War past. The Cane Pace has been hosted since 1997. That race is the first jewel of the Pacing Triple Crown, which includes the Little Brown Jug and Messenger Stakes. Freehold Raceway has kept pace with technology. On any given day or night, you can visit and enjoy thoroughbred and harness racing simulcasts from tracks throughout North America.

Horseracing was part of a growing industry that provided leisure time activities to a community that was finding more and more free time to devote to recreation. A small article in the June 12, 1856 *Monmouth Democrat* provided a glimpse into some other pastimes:

> Mr. William Middleton has opened his New Ice Cream Saloon on South Street. It is fitted up in good style and stocked with an extensive assortment of Confectionery, Fruit, &c. The beaux of our village have no longer an excuse for not treating their sweethearts to Ice Creams, these warm evenings, for Mr. Middleton has fitted up a room for their express accommodation, with tables, chairs, lounges, looking glasses, and all the *et-ceteras*, and keeps a constant supply of Ice Cream, Mineral Water, Cakes, and Candies. Read his advertisement and give him a call.

HARNESS BEAUTY. Earle Avery drives Meadow Skipper to the finish line at Freehold Raceway. (Courtesy of Freehold Raceway Collection.)

As the boundaries and political structure of Freehold changed in the mid- to late-nineteenth century, the Township and the Borough felt the effects of progress. There were changes in commercial activities and changes in transportation—specifically the arrival of the railroad. An anonymous article published in the June 12, 1856 *Monmouth Democrat* applauded the development that had taken place in the township, highlighting the railroad as the impetus to progress:

> The steam engine with its train of advantages, heavily freighted with good fruits, has at length penetrated into this region of county, has viewed its great advantages for improvement, its wealth in resources of good to others— and now regularly plies this agent of advancement. The name of Freehold long ago only known to historians as the battlefield, and to Presbyterians as the residence of Wm. Tennent, is now carried on the tongues of New York merchants. The farmers throughout New Jersey look upon Monmouth Co. as the California of our State, the redeemer of the barrenness of our soul—so rich in marl more valuable really than gold.

CENTRAL RAILROAD STATION. By the end of the nineteenth century, several railroads served Freehold. This is one of the stops along the Central Railroad line. (Courtesy of Monmouth County Historical Association Library and Archives.)

Railroads were constructed primarily to transport produce. They were essential to moving marl and farm-fresh produce throughout the garden state and to the rest of the country. In time, the railroads grew to be an integral part of Freehold's industrial activities as well, moving raw materials and finished products from manufacturers to distant markets. They also became a quick and inexpensive means of transportation for passengers throughout the state. Travel that had previously taken days was accomplished in mere hours.

The Freehold & Keyport Railroad Company, one of the first railroad companies to serve the area, was established on March 2, 1848 by an act of state legislature. The directors of the line were John B. Foreman, Daniel D. Denise, and William D. Davis. The legislature required the company to complete the rails by June 4, 1858 and when opened, the F&K provided a faster means of traveling from inland Freehold to coastal Keyport.

Farmers throughout the state had begun using marl in the late eighteenth century and the industry flourished throughout the nineteenth century. An article in the May 26, 1859 *Monmouth Democrat* gave testimony to the astounding affects of the fertilizer:

> A tract of what is now three farms lying west of the village, and containing over 300 acres, were not readily sold some 20 or 25 years ago for $10 per acre. The smallest of the three containing about 100 acres, and on which are quite old buildings, has been refused for $18,000. From $10 to $180 per acre for a farm together and for farming purposes, in a quarter of a century is something of a rise.
>
> Marl is the great fertilizer here, and has done all this. It exists in great abundance and is of excellent quality. It is carted in all directions as far as that will pay, and large quantities are taken from here by the railroad.

At the 90th session of the New Jersey Legislature, an act was passed and approved on March 22, 1866 to charter the Squankum Railroad & Marl Company. Its corporators were John D. Buckelew, Charles Butcher, Francis H. Holmes, Peter Cortelyou, Samuel T. Williams, Joel Parker, and Robert F. Stockton Jr. The law gave the president and directors the authority to build a railroad that could connect to the Freehold & Jamesburg Agricultural Railroad, the Raritan & Delaware Bay Railroad, or both. The company was allowed to own and transport marl and was given the responsibility to build and maintain roads to facilitate public travel through and around the company property. After 50 years, the roads were to be reassessed. On March 28, 1866, another act was passed that expanded the rights of the Squankum Railroad & Marl Company to extend the railroad across the public highway at Manassee Mill in Howell Township.

According to the Squankum & Freehold Marl Company's Almanac of 1869, the line was complete and ready to begin transporting marl, which it marketed as Green Sand Marl. The railroad extended from the marl pits at Squankum to Freehold Village, about eight miles away. It connected with the Freehold &

Jamesburg branch of the Camden & Amboy Railroad. From Jamesburg, connections were made to all the major railroad lines in New Jersey, including the Belvidere Delaware, Morris & Essex, New Jersey Central, and South Amboy lines. The last line connected to the New York region lines, so Freehold's marl was capable of being delivered to a very large area. The superior quality of Freehold marl, the advanced machinery for processing the fertilizer, and the railroad provided all the necessary ingredients for a successful operation. The Squankum & Freehold Marl Company transported 2 million bushels of Green Sand Marl per year.

The Monmouth County Agricultural Railroad Company was incorporated on April 5, 1867 by an act of legislation. It was empowered to build a railroad from Freehold, by way of the village, to Matawan and to the village of Keyport. Financial problems delayed the completion of the route, but in 1900, the link was completed along with a passenger depot on the southeast corner of Jackson and Mechanic Streets. The Freehold & New York Railroad absorbed both the Monmouth County Agricultural Railroad and the Squankum & Freehold Railroad in July 1877. It later became part of the Central Railroad of New Jersey. Today, its tracks lay abandoned, but its passenger depot is still used as offices.

Prior to 1867, the Freehold & Squankum Railroad and the Farmingdale & Squan Village Railroad connected Wall, Howell, Freehold, and Manalapan. The line of the Farmingdale & Squan Village Railroad was completed and reached beyond Farmingdale in 1853. It arrived in Squan Beach in 1872. Squankum is located about 5 miles northwest of Manasquan and was the terminus of the Freehold & Squankum Railroad.

The Freehold & Jamesburg Agricultural Railroad was chartered in 1851 as a subsidiary of the Pennsylvania Railroad and connected to the primary rail line of the Camden & Amboy Railroad in Jamesburg. Its main purpose was to move marl via connections to the Squankum Railroad and Marl Company, which was chartered in 1866 and merged with the Farmingdale & Squan Village Railroad Company c. 1868–1879. Realizing the need to move travelers along the line, the F&JA started passenger service in 1853. A passenger depot was built c. 1890 on the northwest corner of West Main Street and Throckmorton. In 1981, the building was converted into a bus terminal. The F&JA was absorbed by Conrail.

Other lines that serviced the Freehold area included the Freehold & New York Railroad, which connected Freehold to Matawan with connections to New York & Long Branch Railroad. The Pemberton and Hightstown Railroad made connections to Freehold. New Jersey Central's Southern Division and the Pennsylvania Railroad took over most of New Jersey's lines. It was subsequently bought by Conrail, which became Conrail Shared Assets, an agent for owners CSX and Norfolk Southern Railroad. On January 10, 1890, The Freehold & Keyport Railroad Company merged with the Atlantic Highlands Railroad Company and became known as the Freehold & Atlantic Highlands Railroad Company. This facilitated a continuous line from Freehold to Keyport and then on to the Navesink River.

In addition to railroads, a system of roads was also developed. By the nineteenth century, the Lenni Lenape foot paths had long since faded into a system of roadways leading to farms, mills, churches, and county seats such as Freehold. These roadways were uneven, rutted, and bumpy. Rain and snow caused them to turn to mud, making passage virtually impossible at times. One of the first improvements to the roadways was the use of gravel or stones. By the mid-1800s, groups of investors formed corporations to maintain the roadways. Tollhouses sprang up along major roadways such as the Burlington Path (present day Route 537). Travelers had to stop and pay the toll to the collector, who would distribute the profits to the shareholders.

Another major improvement to New Jersey's transportation system was the introduction of plank roads. Plank roads had been built from the early 1800s and gained popularity by 1830. They were constructed of 3-inch-thick planks installed on the roadway crosswise over three to five stringers, which were buried in the roadbed. The Monmouth County Plank Road Company, which was established on February 20, 1850, built the longest of its kind. It was constructed along the existing road that connected Freehold to Keyport. In 1855, it was authorized to

TOLL HOUSE. *By the mid-1800s, travelers along toll roads had to stop at a house like this to pay a fee for using the road. (Courtesy of Nancy DuBois Wood.)*

take over both the original public road and the Freehold & Keyport Plank Road and convert them to a turnpike. Other plank roads that ran through Freehold were the Freehold & Colts Neck, Freehold & Howell, South River & Freehold, and Monmouth County Plank roads.

Despite the improved conditions brought about by gravel, stone, and planks, the roads in Freehold were criticized by a resident in the May 26, 1859 *Monmouth Democrat*:

> The streets the past winter have been next to impassable, and at some points the side walks not much better. . . . Some of the most public spirited of the inhabitants are replacing the plank walks, laid a few years ago, and which soon become worthless, with flagging of very fine size and quality. South Street has a first rate walk on one side its entire length. Main street has a variety—plank preponderates, while stone and mud are about equal. Altogether there is room for very decided improvement.

Maps have always been important to travelers, but they are also useful to historians by providing other types of information. Recently, the Monmouth County Planning Board reproduced an 1855 map of Freehold originally "surveyed and published by Ezra A. Osborn Surveyor & Conveyancer Middletown New Jersey and Thomas A. Hurley Freehold N.J." It is filled with pieces of Freehold's history, such as daguerreotypes of several residences and businesses—signifying their importance to the community at the time the map was created. There is also a short description of the town and a list of subscribers with their names and occupations. Captions identify the principals of the Freehold Institute as O.R. Willis and A.M. and C.A. Walters. The principal of the Freehold Seminary for Young Ladies was A. Richardson. William I. Patterson & Son were "Merchant Tailors," while Allen, Combs & Co. were a lumber and building materials supplier. Orrin Pharo was the proprietor of the *Monmouth Inquirer*, Isaac S. Buckelew was the superintendent of the Rail Road Depot, and Welch and Carson were the proprietors of the Union Hotel. The map shows what Dr. A.V. Conover's office building and Cowart & Patterson's Dry Goods Store looked like, as well as the residences of the Honorable William H. Conover and John R. Haley, Esq. The courthouse is also depicted. The map clearly highlights Main Street as the heart of Freehold and labels buildings along it as well as South Street, McLean Avenue, Broadway, and Throckmorton where it intersects Main. The inset of the map provides a description of Freehold:

> Freehold, the County Town of Monmouth County, is pleasantly situated within two miles of the Battle Ground, at the Terminus of the Freehold and Jamesburgh Agricultural Railroad, and upon the line of Travel from the Cities of New York and Philadelphia to Long Branch and the other prominent watering-places in the County. It is noted for

94

great Business activity, the excellence of its seminaries of learning, beauty of appearance, its social qualities, and revolutionary history. It has an extensive trade in marl from the famous Squancum Pits, with different parts of the State; the surrounding country is rich in agricultural resources, and both as a place of Business and Residence, Freehold is unsurpassed.

It is fifty miles from New York by Railroad and Steamboat, fifty miles from Philadelphia by Railroad and Steamboat, and sixteen miles from Long Branch, Manasquan and Deal.

In 1854, the Monmouth County Agricultural Society was established. Stock certificates dated 1858 on file at the Monmouth County Historical Association list the following men as stockholders: Thomas S. Barkalow, T.V. DuBois, Charles J. Hendrickson, William H. Hendrickson, Holmes W. Murphy, Ezra O. Osborn, Christopher Probasco, J.E. Ralph, Isaac G. Smock, Tunis Forman Taylor, Daniel P. Van Dorn, and Edmund T. Williams. Each man held one share. The society was a community group that encouraged farmers to use scientific techniques and promoted social interaction. Local farmers also needed a unified voice in area politics. In 1884, a number of the more progressive farmers formed the Monmouth County Board of Agriculture. (This was the group that organized the

WEST FREEHOLD SCHOOL, WEMROCK ROAD, 2002. Another early Freehold Township school, it has been restored by the Freehold Township Historic Preservation Commission.

agricultural fair that became the start of Freehold Raceway.) This group had fewer than 100 members and met about 4 times a year to discuss problems and concerns regarding their farming operations. By 1887, the board had the authority to appoint delegates to the New Jersey State Board of Agriculture, but that influence began to wane by 1910.

As the nation entered World War I, the Monmouth County Board of Agriculture took on a new role as the sponsor of programs designed to encourage thrift and efficiency in farm households. These programs were run by a female agent and geared towards women. By 1921, they expanded to include "club work" among children. This was the precursor to the 4-H Club. Today, the Monmouth County Board of Agriculture is backed by the New Jersey State Board of Agriculture and has the cooperation of Rutgers Agricultural College. It is affiliated with the United States Department of Agriculture and continues to serve the farming community as an outlet for information on scientific farming and technological advancements that affect rural life.

With churches, schools, transportation, agricultural and industrial advances, and leisure activities, the people of Freehold knew that their town could provide all the necessities of a high quality of life. On May 6, 1859, a *Monmouth Democrat* editor gave this statement regarding Freehold's development:

> If we would have our village grow, we must carry on the work of improvement, and never rest until we can offer better inducements to settlers than neighboring villages can. The fact is, in point of location, there is not another town in this section that possesses such advantages. Surrounded with a rich agricultural country, cheap, easy, and speedy access to the city of New York, cheap building lots, low taxes, excellent schools, good water, and Gas Works, we present unequalled inducements for the citizen who wishes to escape from the din and turmoil of the city, and for the manufacturer of light wares, for city trade.

All the town's residents had to do was keep a steady pace of improvement and development, but their American dream was soon shattered by the Civil War. The landscape and attitude of Freehold again changed as much as it had nearly a century earlier, as a result the Revolutionary War.

8. CIVIL WAR: THE BEGINNING OF A NEW ERA

The issues of slavery and state's rights became heated arguments that ultimately provoked the Civil War. As the United States prepared for the conflict, Freehold stood ready to do its part. New Jersey raised over 88,000 troops, mustered and trained in 10 different camps around the state. When President Abraham Lincoln called for volunteers to serve in the Union Army, three regiments were formed of men from Freehold. The new recruits reported to a training camp near the site of the Revolutionary War Battle of Monmouth. The camp was designated Rendezvous Number 3, but was known as Camp Vredenburgh in honor of Judge Peter Vredenburgh Sr.

Camp Vredenburgh was located about 2.5 miles west of the current-day Freehold business district within Monmouth Battlefield State Park on property that was leased to the State of New Jersey by Jacob Herbert. The "Map of Englishtown, New Jersey, 1857 to 1865–68, Not to Scale, Drawn by H. Lansing Perrine, Allenhurst, N.J., October 1905" locates the camp "at a position south of the Freehold & Jamesburg Agricultural Railroad, slightly west of what appears to be the boundary between Manalapan and Freehold Townships. It is southwest of a farmhouse attributed to Charles Jewel, and south of the present Cobb House."

Construction began on July 22, 1862. Wooden barracks were built throughout to lodge the officers, while the enlisted camped in Sibley tents (conical tents resembling tepees). There was space for a stove in the center of the tent with room for 16 men to bunk. There was a railroad stop with an uncovered platform near the camp's main entrance, used to transport soldiers to Trenton and points further south. The camp also had a police system, guardhouse, and stockade. A picket guard was under orders not to let anyone enter or leave the camp without a pass. The cook was in charge of the cookhouse, which provided meals of beef, pork, bread, beans, sugar, and coffee. Local farmers provided fresh beef, wood, and straw. There was also a parade ground that measured over 3 acres. The camp was also equipped with other necessary outbuildings such as a hospital, sinks, and latrines. No battles were fought at the camp; it was a place to muster the troops, train them, and ship them out to fight for the Union Army.

MAJOR PETER VREDENBURGH'S GRAVEMARKER. Originally buried on the battlefield at Opequan, Virginia, Major Vredenburgh's body was disinterred and buried at Maplewood Cemetery in Freehold on September 10, 1864.

The 14th Regiment New Jersey Infantry became the first of five New Jersey regiments to fight in the Civil War. The 14th New Jersey was mustered into service at Camp Vredenburgh on August 26, 1862 and served for nine months. Companies A, D, and G were from Monmouth County including Freehold natives. Like most Union soldiers, Monmouth County volunteers came from all walks of life. They were farmers, clerks, and factory workers. Some joined to avenge the injuries or death of family or friends who served before them. Others acted out of patriotic pride or for bounties from the Federal or local government. Some young men searched for excitement.

Colonel William S. Truex and later, General Charles Haight, commanded the 14th New Jersey. On September 2, 1862 the regiment was ordered to Frederick City, Maryland. Their journey began on cars of the Freehold & Jamesburg Agricultural Railroad, but not before many of them took wives. The September 4th *Monmouth Democrat* reported that "there was a run on marriages in Freehold during the last week of August." After tearful goodbyes, the men shipped out on a journey that took them through Trenton, Philadelphia, and on to Baltimore, where they awaited orders. Their assignment came and they headed for Monocacy Junction near Frederick, Maryland. On September 4, they arrived and began their service guarding the bridge. During the first winter, 31 men died and were buried in Mount Olive Cemetery in Frederick. The bodies of other soldiers were sent home for burial in their native soil. While stationed at Monocacy, some of the companies of the 14th New Jersey were ordered to serve with the Army of the Potomac. In the spring of 1863, they joined the main army and fought in various battles throughout the war.

On May 12, 1863, the men of the 14th New Jersey began their journey home. They reached Washington, D.C. on June 1 and were mustered out of service on June 10 at Halls Hill, Virginia. The diminished regiment arrived in Trenton on June 21. Of the 950 men who left with the 14th New Jersey on September 2, 1862, only 230 returned. The sacrifices made by the 14th were not forgotten; a monument was dedicated to their memory on July 11, 1907 on the banks of the Monocacy River.

On July 28, 1862, Freehold native William Burroughs Ross enlisted in the 14th New Jersey. He was assigned to the Army's Division Headquarters of the 3rd Division, serving under General Washington Lafayette Elliott at Brandy Station in

VREDENBURGH HOUSE. The home of Judge Peter Vredenburgh—father of Civil War hero Major Peter Vredenburgh—is located on Park Avenue and West Main Street in Freehold Borough. This photo was taken by John A. Lloyd on February 5, 1956. (Courtesy of Freehold Public Library.)

Virginia. Ross was promoted from private to sergeant major on January 20, 1864 and later that year, on September 14, he was promoted once again to first lieutenant. He was at the battles of Chancellorsville, Wilderness, Spotsylvania, Cold Harbor, Monocacy, Opequan, and Cedar Creek. First Lieutenant Ross lost his life at the battle of Cedar Creek on October 19, 1864, having served the Union Army over two years.

Another of Freehold's more prominent heroes of the Civil War was Peter Vredenburgh Jr. The son of Judge Peter Vredenburgh Sr. (1805–1873) and Eleanor Brinckerhoff Vredenburgh, he was born on September 12, 1837. He studied law, was admitted to the New Jersey bar in February 1859, and set up practice in Eatontown. On August 25, 1862, he was commissioned by the U.S. Army to serve as a major in the 14th Regiment of the New Jersey Volunteers. Major Vredenburgh served in several capacities during his military career. He was

14TH REGIMENT OF NEW JERSEY VOLUNTEERS REMEMBERED. This monument was erected on April 11, 1907 to honor the 14th NJ and the role it played in the Battle of Monocacy on July 9, 1864. (Courtesy of Monmouth County Historical Association Library and Archives.)

provost marshall, inspector general of the 3rd Division of the 3rd Corps of the 14th Regiment, and served on the staffs of General Washington Lafayette Elliott and General Joseph Bradford Carr. He was then appointed inspector general of the 3rd Corps, consisting of 27,000 soldiers. On March 25, 1864, the 3rd Corps was transferred to the 6th Corps and Major Vredenburgh was assigned to the staff of General James B. Ricketts at headquarters.

Major Vredenburgh fought at a number of military engagements. In 1863, he was at Manassa Gap, Wapping Heights, Culpeper, Bristow Station, Kelly's Ford, Brady Station, Locust Grove, and Mine Run. The following year, he was at Culpeper Ford, Wilderness, Spotsylvania, Spotsylvania Court House, Po River, North Anna, Tolopotomoy, Hanover Court House, Cold Harbor, Bermuda Hundres, Monocacy River, Snicker's Gap, Strasburg, Charlestown, and Opequan—his final battle. On July 9, 1864, Major Vredenburgh requested a transfer from the staff of General Ricketts. His request was granted on August 24, 1864 and he was sent back to the 14th New Jersey. The major was given command of the 14th Regiment for the Battle of Opequan near Winchester, Virginia on September 19, 1864. It was here that he received a mortal wound. He was buried on the battlefield and his body was later disinterred and brought to Freehold, where he was buried on September 30, 1864 in the Maplewood Cemetery.

With no end to the war in sight and more recruits needed to replenish the Union Army, in August 1862, President Abraham Lincoln called for 300,000 volunteers to serve for nine months. Throughout the northern states, regiments organized and marched off to war. Thirty-seven regiments came from New Jersey and two of those formed in Freehold. The first to organize at Camp Vredenburgh in response to President Lincoln's call was the 28th New Jersey under the command of Colonel Moses Wisewell and Lieutenant Colonel Edward A.L. Roberts. Company A was made up of men from Middlesex and Monmouth County. The 28th New Jersey mustered into service on September 22, 1862 with 940 men. On October 4, 1862, they left New Jersey and arrived in Washington, D.C. the next day. Throughout their enlistment, they worked on the defenses at Washington and fought in the battles of Fredericksburg and Chancellorsville. The 28th New Jersey returned to Freehold on June 20 and was mustered out of service on July 6. Their unfortunate claim to fame is that they lost the highest number of men of any nine-month enlisted regiment in the state.

The men of the 29th Regiment of New Jersey Volunteers mustered into service on September 20, 1862 at Camp Vredenburgh—two days before the 28th New Jersey. The 29th was made up of 11 companies (A-K) under the command of Colonel Edwin F. Applegate and Lieutenant Colonel William B. Taylor. The unit consisted of men from Monmouth and Ocean Counties. One company, E, included men from Freehold and Middletown. The regiment left Camp Vredenburgh on Sunday, September 28, 1862. Like the 28th New Jersey, their destination was Washington, D.C. When they arrived on September 30, they were assigned to serve with the Army of the Potomac in the Military Construction Corp and on picket duty on Harper's Ferry Road. They remained in Washington near Tenlytown for several weeks before being ordered to Aquia Creek, Virginia. According to a letter to Major James S. Yard, editor of the *Monmouth Democrat*, the march from Washington to Aquia Creek was long and trying. By December 19, 1862, the regiment reached Aquia Creek. Five companies, including Company E, were given the detail of guarding the railroad at Aquia Landing, about 8 miles away.

During the nine months that the 29th served, letters from the soldiers to family and friends in Freehold, as well as correspondent reports, were published in local newspapers. These letters and reports not only help to track the movement of the 29th, but also tell the story of our nation's Civil War through the eyes of Freehold men. Captain Albert S. Cloke, a correspondent from the *Monmouth Herald and Inquirer*, wrote on February 14, 1863 from a camp near Belle Plains, Virginia that Lieutenant Conk of Freehold had received an honorable discharge due to illness. On March 23, 1863, an article in the *Monmouth Democrat* written by an unidentified reporter stated their location at Camp Potomac near Pratt's Point, Virginia and that Sergeant Major Bob Miller had been made second lieutenant of Company E.

One of the more uplifting experiences for Union soldiers was the welcome visit of the paymaster. The following excerpt was written by an unknown correspondent on April 26, 1863 at Camp Paul near Belle Plains, Virginia and published in the May 7, 1863 *Monmouth Democrat*. It captures the atmosphere of payday in a Civil War Union camp:

> The long looked for Paymaster arrived in camp yesterday, and his coming was received with joy by all hands. We were paid for four months. Jonathan Cook, Esq., of Trenton, was here at the same time, and the regiment sent home by him to their families and friends the snug little sum of thirty-three thousand nine hundred dollars ($33,900). The largest sum sent from any one company was $3,880 sent by Co. G of Holmdel. Co. E. of Freehold sent $3,337. Don't you think that is doing remarkably well?

On June 16, 1863, the 29th Regiment was ordered to return to Freehold. As they marched home, they left behind the Army of the Potomac, who shortly afterwards met on a battlefield in Gettysburg, Pennsylvania. The 29th was not part of this historic battle, but they had done their part in support of the Union and were greeted with a grand parade and reception at the Freehold Fairgrounds after they returned home on June 16, 1863. The following excerpt from an article in the June 28, 1863 *Monmouth Democrat* captures the mood of the town and the soldiers as they celebrated the return of the 29th:

> At an early hour on Saturday morning, the citizens of the county began to pour in from every township. At 9 o'clock the Wall Guards arrived and were escorted to their quarters by the Freehold Infantry. The

McClellan Guards arrived shortly after, and after them came the Governor's Light Guard, the Holmdel Infantry and the Raritan Guard—the three latter companies under command of Capt. Wm. B. Forman, senior officer of the 4th Regt. The line was formed shortly after 10 o'clock on Throckmorton avenue, the right resting on the Railroad depot. While the line was forming, a special train of cars arrived with the Twenty-Ninth. They were received by the volunteer militia, and were then escorted to the Fair Grounds. . . .

To describe the warm greetings, and happy re-unions which took place on this occasion, would require a more facile pen than ours. Suffice it, that among the thousands of faces present there were none but were wreathed with smiles—the bronzed and travel-stained soldier happy that his feet were again on his native soil, and the parents and wives, and children and friends, all glad to welcome them home again.

The entire route of the procession—down Throckmorton Street to Main Street, and up Main Street directly to the fair ground—was densely packed with people. As the head of the column came in sight of the fair ground, the Parker Artillery—who were stationed there—fired a salute from their guns, which had

GOVERNOR PARKER'S RESIDENCE, 1906–1907. This is Governor Parker's residence as it appeared almost 20 years after his death in 1888. (Courtesy of Freehold Public Library.)

arrived only a day or two before. As the procession entered the fair grounds, cheer after cheer burst from the assembled multitude. The soldiers were drawn up inside of a circle of well-wishers opposite the music stand. Reverend Frank Chandler led the prayer, Reverend W.W. Christine read a letter from Governor Parker, and Reverend John W. Kramer provided the reception address. At the conclusion, Colonel Taylor briefly responded and called upon the regiment to evince their appreciation with three "old-fashioned Virginia cheers," which were given heartily.

The 29th was then escorted by the township committeemen to the large exhibition building of the Agricultural Society, where a bountiful feast—composed of as great a variety of eatables as could be procured—was spread. The provisions were furnished by the central committee and cooked under their supervision, but the tables were set by a volunteer committee of ladies, led by the patriotic wife of the governor. The ladies served the meal, assisted by committeemen from the several townships. There was plenty of food for the military, with enough left over to afford a "bite" for the hundreds who had been delayed by the proceedings beyond their usual dinner hour. After, Colonel Taylor furloughed his men until Tuesday morning and before 6:00 p.m., the town was pretty well cleared of soldiers and visitors.

The 29th New Jersey was mustered out of service on June 28, 1863, the last to do so from Camp Vredenburgh. The camp that had for eighteen months sent thousands of Freehold men to defend the cause of the Union soon reverted to farmland. Late in January 1864, its buildings were dismantled and shipped to Trenton. Its three regiments are remembered in the pages of newspapers and history books and articles. Although there is no visible evidence of Camp Vredenburgh today, it is a proud part of Freehold's history.

Freehold's connection to the Civil War reached beyond the boundaries of Camp Vredenburgh. One of the finest commissioned officers was a native of Freehold, Joel Parker, who served as brigadier general and major general from 1857 to 1861. Parker was born on November 24, 1816 in a house on the Mount Holly road about 4 miles west of Freehold in what is now Millstone Township. When he was five years old, his family moved to Trenton. He was educated at the old Trenton Academy, Lawrenceville High School, and Princeton University. After graduating in 1839, he studied law under the Honorable Henry W. Green of Trenton and was admitted to the bar in 1842. He married Maria M. Gummere the following year. The Parkers settled in Freehold and Joel began his political career.

Parker was a Freemason and an honorary member of the Society of the Cincinnati. He became a Democratic speaker in 1844 and served as a member of the House of Assembly in 1848. He served one term as Prosecutor of the Pleas of Monmouth from 1852 to 1857. Parker's military service began in 1857, when he was appointed brigadier general of the Monmouth & Ocean Brigade of the State Militia. On May 7, 1861, he took command of the 3rd Division New Jersey Militia as major general. Shortly after leaving his commissioned post in 1863, he was elected New Jersey's governor. He served in that post from 1863 to 1866 and

GRAVESITE OF JOEL PARKER, 2002. The gravestone that marks Governor Parker's resting place captures the essence of the man with the words "Honored and Beloved."

again from 1872 to 1875. His political career also included service as a presidential elector from 1860 to 1878 and as justice of the Supreme Court of New Jersey from 1780 to 1888. In 1878, Parker was instrumental in helping to raise money for the local monument commemorating the Battle of Monmouth. After serving as governor, he was appointed attorney general of New Jersey, where he served until 1880. In 1881, Parker became a member of the Presbyterian Church of Freehold. On Saturday, December 31, 1887, he fell ill in Philadelphia and went to the house of a friend, Mrs. Cecelia Root. Shortly after he arrived, he suffered a stroke. He went in and out of consciousness until he died on Monday, January 2, 1888.

Joel Parker was one of the most revered governors of the State of New Jersey. Honorable Thomas H. Dudley of Camden summed up Parker's character in a memorial:

Joel Parker was true; he was honest and loyal. He undertook the work and he did it. . . . He was patriotic and gave his hands and his heart to the work. He did his duty and he did it well, and the people sustained him. He was true and loyal to the State and the country, and the oath of office he had taken.

The town of Freehold held a citizen's meeting on the day Governor Parker died and wrote a testimonial in his honor:

As a public-spirited, broad-minded, large-hearted, whole-souled citizen, he was foremost in every enterprise promotive of the social, commercial, educational, and artistic advancement of our community.

As a counselor in the practice of his profession, he was conscientious, industrious and learned, at once an earnest and eloquent advocate, a safe guide and a fearless companion.

As Governor of our State—and notably during the patriotic period of our civil war—he was conspicuous among his contemporaries for ability, probity, loyalty and courage, leading and inspiring the masses.

Joel Parker was laid to rest in historic Maplewood Cemetery on the edge of Freehold Borough. His tombstone is engraved with all his accomplishments, but the essence of the man is captured in the words "Honored and Beloved."

9 EAST MAIN STREET. This was one of the many establishments operating in Freehold Borough in the years following the Civil War. (Courtesy of Freehold Public Library.)

9. FREEHOLD AND RECONSTRUCTION

Following the Civil War, the United States entered a period of reconstruction. Battles fought throughout the states left many areas in desperate need of physical rebuilding. But not only did the buildings and infrastructure of the United States need repair, but the very spirit of the American people needed mending. After the war ended, secession was renounced and political leadership in the south was replaced with northerners. Confederates were not executed for war crimes and their land was not confiscated en masse, but slavery was ended.

The early settlers of Freehold did not rely heavily on slaves to work their farms. In 1771, a census taken by Richard Stout revealed that there were 158 slaves in Freehold and most of these were household servants. In 1784, the number of slaves dropped to 104, but six years later in 1790, the population of Freehold consisted of 3,146 whites, 12 free African Americans, and 627 slaves. Of those 12 free African Americans, one was a farmer named Bunn who owned 100 acres in 1787. He seems to be the only free African American documented to have owned property in Freehold. By 1796, the number of slaves in Freehold had increased by more than 80 percent to approximately 18 percent of the township's population. When New Jersey enacted gradual emancipation in 1804, Freehold was slow to respond. By 1810, the number of slaves actually rose 12 percent to 702. It took an amendment to the United States Constitution to make a real impact on slavery in Freehold. The Thirteenth Amendment was ratified on December 6, 1865. It states that "neither slavery nor involuntary servitude, except as a punishment for crime whereof the party shall have been duly convicted, shall exist within the United States, or any place subject to their jurisdiction."

From the 1840s, African Americans in Freehold had attended separate schools. After the thirteenth amendment, there were some minor attempts to address the issue of education for emancipated slaves. Freehold resident Samuel Lockwood (1819–1894) was a pioneer in this effort. Lockwood was born on January 20, 1819 in Mansfield, Nottinghamshire, England to an affluent family. His family moved to New York when he was a young boy. He graduated from the City University of New York in 1847 and attended the New Jersey Theological Seminary. He was ordained as a Dutch Reformed preacher in 1850 and began his ministry in Cortland, New York. He moved from Cortland to Gibbon, New York and in 1854, moved once again to Keyport, New Jersey, where he accepted a pastorate. Lockwood's work was not confined to preaching. He studied nature and science and made contributions to the fields of microscopy, botany, and zoology. His interests even went beyond religion and science: he was an avid advocate for education.

Two laws were passed to advance the organization of education in New Jersey. In 1865, one established the State Board of Education. In 1867, the other—known as the New School Law—abolished the positions of town superintendent and county examiner, created the State Board of Education, and instituted the office of county superintendent. Lockwood was instrumental in organizing the State Board of Education and served as the state's first county superintendent of schools.

In 1870, Lockwood moved to a house on Broad Street in Freehold. Supported by Captain G.W. Vanderveer, who helped procure the use of the schoolhouse, Lockwood opened a night school for freed slaves from December 12, 1870 to March 10, 1871. He had hoped to sign up nine volunteer teachers, but only Mrs. L.M. Murray, Mr. J.M. Wainwright, and Mr. Benjamin Carpenter came to his aid.

SAMUEL R. FORMAN'S SALES AND EXCHANGE STABLES. *This was where horses and mules were sold and exchanged between 1880 and 1920. Forman left the property to the town to be used as a park. Today it is a parking lot. (Courtesy of Freehold Public Library.)*

FRED A. WHITE PLUMBING AND HARDWARE STORE. This business was located at 48 West Main Street in Freehold Borough. White is in the center of the picture. (Courtesy of Freehold Public Library.)

Despite this disappointment, Lockwood moved forward and organized the classes in the schoolhouse. His only teaching materials were a donation of 50 books from Mr. Peabody of Charles Scribner & Company. When the first session concluded, Lockwood was gratified by the accomplishments of those who attended the Adult Evening School. In a letter to the editor published in the November 23, 1871 *Monmouth Democrat*, Lockwood stated that:

> The desire is general among our colored people to have the school resume, and surely to those who a good providence has blessed with educational advantages, there can hardly be a better opportunity afforded of doing good, than by devoting a part of the evenings of the week to teaching these needy ones.

It took many more years for the African-American community in Freehold to organize an educational facility. In 1915, the Court Street School opened. Originally organized by the Freehold Board of Education as a totally segregated school, its first building was a one-room wood structure. A new one-story brick structure with stone trim was built between 1919 and 1921. It had two classrooms and in 1926, two more rooms were added—one on the front and one on the back of the building. From its beginning in 1915 until the outbreak of World War II, all

BIRCH'S BARGAIN STORE. This business was located in Freehold Borough at 36 West Main Street. (Courtesy of Freehold Public Library.)

of the African-American children living in Freehold attended the Court Street School, which provided education from kindergarten through eighth grade. During WW II, the schoolhouse was used as an air raid shelter and ration station. In 1947, the school reopened as an integrated school for kindergarten through third grade. The school closed in 1974 and was used as Freehold Borough's administration building. It was then sold to Monmouth County and used as a juvenile probation center until 1981. Sometime after that, the building was leased to the Court Street School Board of Trustees, who converted it to a neighborhood center serving the African-American community.

Education was a priority in the years following the Civil War, but not the only one. Municipal services were an important part of the growing community. Over the years, fires had damaged or destroyed the courthouse, jail, and other buildings throughout Freehold, but there was no organized fire company. An article that appeared in the January 10, 1867 *Long Branch News* reported a fire at the Dutch Reformed Church on the previous Saturday at around 1:00 p.m. There was approximately $300 in damage and G.W. Patterson, Esq. and Joseph Betts of New York were slightly burned while helping to fight the fire. The reporter:

. . . heard a few persons speaking favorable to a fire engine, but as the church did not burn down, of course it is not needed. Pails are so much better, and there are so many of them. We do not intend to have any large fires, or else we might consider the question of a fire apparatus, and finally resolve it would be too expensive. Thus we progress.

That fire-fighting equipment was too expensive a proposition for a town that did "not intend to have any large fires" may very well have been the general consensus, because it was four years before the issue was addressed. In the fall of 1871, two meetings were held at Rosell's Hall, but residents could not come to an agreement on the need for fire fighting equipment and nothing was accomplished. However, a third meeting held at the courthouse proved to be more fruitful. Committees were appointed to take on the preliminary work of organizing a fire company. Bylaws, a constitution, and an addendum to the act of incorporation for the township were drafted. The addendum authorized the Board of Commissioners to raise money for fire-fighting equipment, a building to house the fire company, etc. It was passed by the state legislature at its 1872 session.

On April 20, 1872, the Good Will Hook & Ladder Company became a reality. Its constitution was signed by eight commissioners: James J. Conover, A.R. Throckmorton, G.C. Hulett, Charles J. Parker, D.S. Crater, Thomas A. Ward,

GARDNER WOODWARD'S GROCERY STORE. *Woodward supplied Freehold Borough residents with their grocery needs from this humble store at 28 West Main Street. (Courtesy of Freehold Public Library.)*

George B. Cooper, and C.F. Richardson. The company held its first regular monthly meeting on June 6th at Throckmorton's law office. Meetings for the remainder of the year were held monthly at Rosell's Hall. They moved to the courthouse from January 1873 until April. For the next six months, the meetings were once again held in Throckmorton's law office. The November and December meetings took place at Acton Civil Hartshorne's office. From January 1874 through April 1875, the company's headquarters were set up in space located over Mrs. Smock's music store. Finally, in April 1875, the Good Will Hook & Ladder Company moved to its permanent engine house at 57 Throckmorton Street near Broad Street.

GOOD WILL HOOK & LADDER COMPANY. Freehold's long-awaited fire department became a reality in 1872. Here, some of its volunteers are seen in front of the station house c. 1890. (Courtesy of Monmouth County Historical Association Library and Archives.)

FREEHOLD'S GREAT FIRE, OCTOBER 30, 1873. One of the most devastating fires hit Freehold shortly after the Good Will Hook & Ladder Company was organized. The morning after the fire was doused E.B. Bedle, Joseph A. Yard, and David Conover were photographed by Ferris C. Lockwood.

It had taken some time for the residents of Freehold to recognize the need for an organized fire department, but it came just in the nick of time. Eighteen months after the Good Will Hook & Ladder Company came into being, it was called to service in one of the most devastating fires Freehold ever witnessed. On October 30, 1873, fire struck Freehold with a vengeance. The Thursday, November 6, 1873 *Monmouth Inquirer* reported that:

> It appears, then, that our citizens retired to rest on Wednesday night with all that sense of security that usually settles upon our quiet town. It was shortly after midnight when MR. WILLIAM BURRELL, bartender of the Union Hotel was about to go to bed, when glancing out of his bedroom window he saw the *Monmouth Inquirer* building, directly opposite, was on fire. He rushed out to give the alarm and met MR. WILL SANDERS, a clerk in Gen. Haight's law office, which is located in the *Inquirer* building, and together they hastened across the street with a view of saving the General's books and papers.

So began "the greatest public calamity that ever befell our town." A half-hour passed after William Burrell first viewed the fire before Mr. A. Richardson, principal of the Freehold Young Ladies Seminary, rang the school bell alerting the town of the disaster. In a short time, it became apparent that the efforts of Freehold's Good Will Hook & Ladder Company alone were not enough to douse the conflagration, which spread rapidly. An urgent telegraph was transmitted to the New Brunswick, Trenton, and Bordentown fire departments. New Brunswick could not prudently spare its one and only engine. Trenton and Bordentown were ready and willing to help, but needed transportation to the site. Thus, the Freehold Fire Department, led by Chief James J. Conover and Good Will Hook & Ladder Company Foreman G.C. Huelett, had to fight the flames with the support of several courageous residents.

The fire spread through the south and west part of the village, inflicting nearly $100,000 in damage to public and private buildings. The courthouse, jail, post office, offices of the clerk, surrogate, and sheriff, and several businesses—including E.B. Bedles' Dry Goods & Grocery Store, Burtis's Dry Goods & Grocery Store, Conover & Thompsons' Clothing & Furnishings Store, Bodee's Barber Shop, and *The Monmouth Inquirer*—were either destroyed or heavily damaged. As county seat, Freehold had many law offices, several of which sustained damage. William H. Vredenburgh, Esq. perhaps sustained the worst loss of all. In his office was a valuable collection of law books, passed to him from the estates of Daniel B. Ryall and Judge Peter Vredenburgh. Few of the books survived the fire. The Ryall Homestead, owned and occupied by Colonel P.G. Vought and his wife, was totally destroyed. Although it seemed that the entire town would succumb, the hard work and perseverance of the Good Will Hook & Ladder Company and dedicated Freehold residents eventually defeated the flames.

In the end, several factors served to contain and eventually extinguish the fire. The thick walls of the courthouse helped prevent the flames from moving northward. The deliberate destruction by the Hook & Ladder Company of a hundred-year-old building that housed J.W. Schwartz's law office, the Home Sewing Machine Agency, and Dr. W.W. Pitman's dental office helped arrest the flames in the southwest. Finally, the town's shade trees lining its streets provided a hindrance to the spreading of the fire. Their foliage grew close together at their tops and on the evening of the fire, the crisp autumn air was still and the trees caused the flames and fire flakes to move in an upward direction, impeding the fire from spreading to other buildings.

A special meeting of the Board of Chosen Freeholders was held on November 1 at 10:00 a.m. in the Davis Hotel to take the necessary action to restore the public buildings destroyed by the fire. The Board agreed to form a committee responsible for making arrangements for a place to hold court. They also authorized construction of a temporary roof and stairs to the vault of the surrogate's office. This allowed business to be conducted in the courthouse while permanent repairs were completed. Mr. Samuel Sloane served as architect for the

GOOD WILL FIRE ENGINE. At the turn of the twentieth century, the horse-drawn hook and ladder vehicle was replaced with a motorized fire engine. (Courtesy of Monmouth County Historical Association Library and Archives.)

repairs. Stonework from the remains of the original structure was used to construct the new building, which was completed in four months. While the construction was underway, court sessions were conducted in the Dutch Reformed Church.

Unlike previous fires, this one was covered by several insurance policies. A meeting was held between the Freeholders and the insurance agents on November 6, 1873 at 10:00 a.m. in Fleming's Hotel to determine the amount to be issued for the repairs. The agents asked the Freeholders to estimate the amount of damages, but the board was not prepared to do so. The agents thus presented their estimates of $24,929 from Fran H.W. Wilson and $24,200 from Elwood Smith and proposed that Smith be hired. The board refused and adjourned the meeting. At the next board meeting on November 12, Smith proposed that he would accept $24,200 minus a cash discount of $200 to repair the courthouse. After the insurance agents agreed to pay the $24,000 to Smith, the courthouse was repaired.

Several years later, in 1884, the courthouse was expanded by a large addition to its rear on Court Street. Forty-six years later, it once again sustained fire damage. During Reconstruction, from 1875 to 1878, Joseph Dorsett Bedle served as governor of New Jersey. Born into a politically-connected family in Middletown Point (present-day Matawan) on January 5, 1831, Bedle was destined to become a politician. He studied law in Trenton and was admitted to the New Jersey Bar in 1853. After practicing law in Middletown Point for two years, he moved to Freehold and married Althea F. Randolph in 1856. Governor Joel Parker appointed Bedle to the New Jersey Supreme Court in 1865, making him the youngest justice to serve the state's supreme court. Bedle moved to Jersey City to facilitate his work on the Supreme Court, on which he served until being elected governor in 1875.

Bedle believed that a government that allowed its citizens to govern themselves was in the best interest of all. In his inaugural address, the governor stated that "the simpler the machinery of a local government the better." Throughout his term, Bedle held tight to this belief and passed laws reflecting it. Governor Bedle also affected the railroads. In 1877, he called up the New Jersey National Guard to protect the equipment and employees of two railroads that suffered a strike. After serving one term, Bedle returned to his law practice, served as counsel for the Delaware, Lackawanna & Western Railroad, became director of several prominent corporations, and was a member of the constitutional commission of 1894. On October 21, 1894, Bedle died after surgery for the removal of bladder stones. He is buried in Maplewood Cemetery in Freehold.

GRAVESITE OF JOSEPH DORSETT BEDLE, 2002. Governor Bedle is buried in Maplewood Cemetery, not far from Governor Parker.

10. THE INDUSTRIAL REVOLUTION IN FREEHOLD

As the United States continued recovering from the devastation of the Civil War, Freehold kept pace and became immersed in another revolution. The industrial revolution had made its way to the United States from Europe, and with it came new technology for mass production of goods. Several manufacturing companies located their operations in Freehold. Public utilities became available to residents and businesses. Freehold began to take on the form of the township and borough that we know today. Residences and businesses sprang up side by side. Community services such as churches and schools became more readily available.

Throughout all this forward-looking growth, the people of Freehold did not forget the sacrifices made by those who fought for independence and a free, democratic society. The concept of memorializing the heroes of the American Revolution took root prior to the Civil War, but did not come to fruition until many years after. It was unveiled in 1884, but the journey to that day had been a long one, starting in 1846. On June 18 of that year, the *Monmouth Inquirer* printed the following advertisement:

Monument
On
Monmouth Battle-Ground

> The citizens of Monmouth county, who are in favor of taking measures to erect a monument to commemorate the Battle of Monmouth, are requested to meet in the Court House, in the village of Freehold, on SATURDAY, the 27th inst., at 3 o'clock, P.M. *Signed* John Hull, Wm. H. Bennett, Enoch Coward, D.V. McLean, A.C. McLean, J.B. Throckmorton, H.D. Polhemus, B.F. Randolph

The *Monmouth Democrat* published a report of the resulting meeting in the July 2, 1846 issue. It listed the following resolutions proposed by D.V. McLean and adopted by the committee:

1. *Resolved*, That it is the duty of a grateful posterity to commemorate not only in their hearts, but by suitable monuments, the noble deeds of their fathers, and the important events in their history.

2. *Resolved*, That among the important events of our Revolutionary struggle, the Battle of Monmouth should never be forgotten.

3. *Resolved*, That we believe the time has fully come when the citizens of Monmouth County should unite and erect a suitable monument to commemorate that important event.

4. *Resolved*, That the proceedings of this meeting be published in the Freehold papers.

On August 4, another meeting created the Monmouth Battle Monument Association and Commission, but it accomplished nothing for over 20 years. In 1854, an attempt was made to jump-start the process when a former Freehold resident living in Syracuse, New York wrote a letter to the editor of the *Monmouth Democrat*. In it, Major S.S. Forman recalled the movement of 1846 and urged that a monument be erected. Forman's letter may have turned some in favor of building the monument, but it did nothing to stir the association into action.

Then, on June 28, 1877, former Governor Joel Parker gave a speech at the 99th anniversary of the Battle of Monmouth celebration. In September, a preliminary

BATTLE OF MONMOUTH MONUMENT UNVEILING. This announced the unveiling of the monument on November 13, 1884. (Courtesy of Freehold Public Library.)

BATTLE OF MONMOUTH MONUMENT. The monument is located on a triangular piece of land between Court and Monument Streets in front of the courthouse.

meeting was held and on October 2, 1877, a new organization—the Monmouth Battle Monument Association—was created. The Monmouth Monument Association incorporated on May 7, 1878 and quickly began fundraising. Parker, along with Major James S. Yard of the *Monmouth Democrat* and three other men from Monmouth County, were named to the campaign. From 1878 to 1880, New Jerseyans contributed $10,000 to the project.

The heirs of Daniel S. Schanck donated the property for the monument. The triangular piece of land—located on Court Street next to the courthouse and across the street from the Monmouth County Historical Association—was conveyed to the county on February 2, 1878 by Mrs. Mary A. Schanck, Mrs. Theo. W. Morris, Mrs. Alice C. Schanck, Mr. Andrew H. Schanck, Mr. Daniel S. Schanck, and Mr. George S. Schanck. It took six years to raise the $36,000 necessary to complete the monument, but its dedication finally took place on November 13, 1884. The following detailed description is excerpted from the *Memorial of the Committee of Arrangements for the Unveiling of the Monmouth Battle Monument at Freehold, New Jersey*:

The base of the monument is in the form of an equilateral triangle, with canon at each angle. Three spurs of granite form the base of the shaft, surmounted by the point of contact by a large drum-shaped block, on which five bronze reliefs, illustrative of the battle, will be placed. Above the tablets and around the shaft are the coats of arms, in bronze, of the thirteen original states, festooned with laurel leaves. Rising above this is the shaft proper, consisting of three sections, joined by rings of bay leaves. The shaft is surmounted by a composite capital on which is a statue of Columbia Triumphant.

The five bas reliefs represent: Lieutenant Colonel Nathaniel Ramsey holding off the British until General George Washington and the main army would arrive; General Washington rallying the troops; Molly Pitcher replacing her wounded husband as a cannoneer; the Council of War at Hopewell, where Washington met with his senior officers to discuss battle strategies; and General "Mad" Anthony Wayne leading his troops in the final charge of the battle.

The dedication ceremony was reviewed by Governor Leon Abbett and led by several regiments of the New Jersey National Guard, the Committee of Arrangements, and others. After the procession gathered around the monument, Bishop Scarborough read the invocation. Theodore Morris, president of the Committee of Arrangements, then presented the monument to the people of Freehold. Governor Abbett accepted it on their behalf. Speeches were given by

POTATO FARMING IN FREEHOLD. Freehold was known for its farming industry; potatoes were one of the most productive crops. (Courtesy of Freehold Public Library.)

BAWDEN'S FIREPLACE WORKS, c. 1870. An inscription reads: "Business opened in 1856—Freehold Iron Foundry, Proprietor and founder John Bawden is most likely one of the gentlemen in photo, along with partner, Gilbert Combs." (Courtesy of Monmouth County Historical Association Library and Archives.)

such dignitaries as ex-governor Joel Parker. The ceremony concluded with a benediction by Reverend George C. Maddock. An estimated 25,000–30,000 people crowded the dedication ceremony.

The monument to honor those who had fought for U.S. independence was complete and the people of Freehold were beginning to experience the progress of the industrial revolution. Stores and other outlets for selling mass-produced goods became necessary. One of the longest-existing dry goods stores was owned by the Perrine Family, starting with David Clark Perrine.

David was born in Clarksburg in 1816 and moved to Freehold in 1830. As a young man, he worked for Lippincott, Davis & Company, a dry goods supplier. Later, he worked for Cowart & Perrine in the same business. In 1852, after several years of hard work and learning the business, Perrine established his own store on West Main Street in a large brick building. He named the store Perrine's General Merchandise Store, but local residents called it the "Big Red Store." Perrine's thrived in its prime location. Around 1880, David changed the name of his establishment to D.C. Perrine's Dry Goods. Upon David's death in 1888, his son David Vanderveer Perrine ran the store.

THE BIG RED STORE. *D.V. Perrine operated this general store, which was founded by his father, D.C. Perrine. This picture was taken on the West Main Street side of the store. From left to right are: Al Crawford, Sam Hankins, David H. Robinson, Anne Bawden, Angie Buckalew, John M. Voorhees, Addie Wells, Mrs. Charles H. Clayton, Lester Clayton, an unidentified boy, Mr. Charles E. VanDerveer, William T. Ackerman, George Frake, and Steve Long. The original photo was taken c. 1897.*

Business was doing well, when on September 11, 1886 fire broke out at D.C. Perrine's. It started in the paint oil room in the cellar. Smoke escaped through an archway that opened near the adjoining building that housed Taylor's Hotel. (This was the same hotel that had been the Union Tavern in the early 1800s.) Before long, the fire spread to Taylor's and move rapidly down Main Street for about 100 feet to the corner of South Street. Volunteers helped Taylor move furniture from his hotel to the lawn in front of the courthouse, but despite their efforts, most of it was badly damaged or destroyed. At the time, there were no hydrants in Freehold and fighting the fire became too risky, so the decision was made to abandon the fight for the hotel.

In the end, one barn and seven stores—including the long-established Taylor's Hotel—were destroyed. The hotel was valued at about $15,000 and John Taylor had $10,000 in insurance on the building, $5,000 for furniture, and $1,500 for outbuildings. Taylor moved his family into the home of Mrs. Vredenburgh on Main Street opposite the Dutch Reformed Church and set about planning the reconstruction of his hotel. After the hotel was rebuilt, Taylor operated it for a few more years. In 1888, it was renovated and replaced by the Belmont Hotel. The Belmont Hotel served Freehold for 45 years before it also succumbed to fire.

In February 1933, Freehold was once again set ablaze with a spectacular fire. Although the temperature was far below freezing, the conflagration was intense enough to warrant the help of four fire companies: from Freehold, Englishtown, Adelphia, and Lakewood. Fortunately, fire fighters were able to subdue the blaze, but it took two days for road department workers equipped with ice picks and shovels to clear the area of the 4-to-8-inch thick ice that had formed on the hoses and streets. When the smoke and ice cleared, damage to the Belmont Hotel was estimated at over $100,000.

During this period of industrial development, Americans experienced more and more time for leisure activities, such as bicycling. Freeholder Arthur Z. Zimmerman was a bicycle fanatic who opened a small bicycle manufacturing company, Arthur Z. Zimmerman Manufacturing Company (also known as Burtis & Zimmerman Manufacturing Company) at 19 Elm Street in Freehold Borough *c.* 1889. There, Zimmerman perfected his "Zimmy" bicycle and manufactured it for the public. By 1901, Zimmerman moved his company out of Freehold, leaving the building vacant. It was subsequently used by the Wilbur Stephens Company Shirt Factory *c.* 1909 and by clothing manufacturer Sigmund Eisner Company between World War I through the 1920s.

ADOLPH DITTMAR BAKERY, c. 1900–1905. The bakery was located at 11 South Street in Freehold Borough. (Courtesy of Freehold Public Library.)

Another pastime of Freeholders in the late nineteenth century was attending performances and lectures of writers, artists, and actors. On Monday, May 10, 1882, Shinn's Hall presented a lecture on "The English Renaissance" by the controversial Oscar Wilde. The event was publicized by a reporter from the May 4th *Monmouth Democrat*:

> Mr. Wilde has been the subject of a great deal of newspaper gossip, and the object of the small wits of the press both in England and America, and many people do not really understand whether much of what has been said was fun or earnest. The facts are that he is a quiet, unobtrusive gentleman who has made the beautiful in art his study, and has something practical to say about it that practical everyday people may profit by as well as the select few.

Contrary to the reporter's wishes that Wilde be received warmly by an abundant audience, the lecture was reportedly a disaster. Wilde, the "apostle of aestheticism," made a buffoon of himself. His outlandish apparel, long hair, and effeminate ways were not well received by the Freehold audience. His lecture was described by the May 11, 1882 *Monmouth Democrat* as "very fine, his word painting was grand, his diction choice. But his delivery was poor; he mouthed his words; his elocution was simply offensive." What might have been a grand intellectual

73 SOUTH STREET, c. 1905. Now the Vansant Funeral Home, this home was previously owned by undertaker David L. Clayton. (Courtesy of Freehold Public Library.)

BROADWAY AND EAST MAIN STREET, AUGUST 15, 1906. This is what the intersection of Route 79 (Broadway) and Route 537 (East Main Street) looked like about 100 years ago. Today the intersection holds a memorial to those who sacrificed their lives in World War II. (Courtesy of Freehold Public Library.)

occasion turned out to be a literary flop. Regardless, events like Wilde's lecture became more commonplace in a community that—as a result of the industrial revolution—had more time to spend on leisure activities. New businesses also sprang up to complement the advancing technology that became part of everyday life in Freehold.

In the spring of 1882, Brakeley's Canning Factory was established by Joseph Brakeley (1852–1937), the son of Asher Brakeley of Bordentown. Joseph had worked at his father's canning factory before moving to Freehold and opening his own business. Joseph was an enterprising and innovative man. Besides his success in the canning business, he is credited with inventing pea and bean shellers and sorters. Brakeley's Canning Factory was located on the northwest corner of Manalapan and Bowne Avenues and originally consisted of three buildings. There was a 40-foot-square, one-story factory building; a 20-by-20-foot, two-story tin shop, where they manufactured the tin used to make cans for storing the produce; and a 26-by-52-foot, two-story warehouse. In its first year of operation, approximately 50 people were employed, mostly women. According to the October 11, 1883 *Monmouth Democrat,* the payroll was "not less than sixty dollars per day, the women earning about one dollar a day each, and the men in proportion." Brakeley also provided a barracks for seasonal workers.

HOLMES HOME, 49 WEST MAIN STREET. Nellie and Ann Conover stand on the porch of the home where their half brother William S. Holmes was born in 1876. William was the first mayor of Freehold Borough (1919–1926). The home was cut apart in 1915 to make way for a new building for the fire and police departments. The two sections of the original home were relocated to 52 West George Street and 23 Yard Avenue. (Courtesy of Freehold Public Library.)

In its first year of business, Brakeley's canned tomatoes. Later, it added spinach, peas, and beans. The first year's crop was negatively affected by poor spring and summer weather in 1882 and the canning operation fell far short of its 10,000-cans-per-day capacity. Still, Brakeley was optimistic and planned to enlarge the size of his buildings and the amount of fruit he purchased the next season. He also planned to expand his products to include pumpkins, corn, and peas.

An article in the October 11, 1883 *Monmouth Democrat* gave a detailed description of the canning facility and process. It ended with a very uplifting message:

> We are glad that there are such men as Mr. Brakeley, who, having the capital and the experience, are not afraid to risk them in enterprises of this kind. We happen to know by the experience of others that this business is peculiarly uncertain, having more than the ordinary business risks attending it, and so we are disposed to give Mr. Brakeley the more praise for his bravery, and to heartily commend him for his enterprise, and to wish him that success that will enable him to greatly enlarge it.

Those good wishes were manifested by Brakeley's success. Between 1890 and 1920, his factory was expanded as Brakeley had planned and the business did as well as he had hoped. There were two major physical additions during this period: the canning house was enlarged in 1903 and the warehouse was expanded between 1901 and 1908. The latter addition included a new office and storage sheds.

Things looked good for Brakeley and his business prospered. Then, 40 years later, the canning factory fell on hard times. When a rare disease attacked the vines and made it unprofitable to continue producing peas, Brakeley began growing lima beans. The company did well until the bean crop was affected by mildew and failed for two straight years (1926 and 1927), causing financial difficulties. In September 1927, Brakeley closed the factory for an early vacation for his employees, who were accustomed to having such time off in the late fall. The next month, he began selling off hundreds of acres of farmland. By early December, the farm on the Colt's Neck Road was sold to Clarence Wilson. Then the 181-acre Parsonage farm on the Freehold-Englishtown Road was sold to Charles Applegate for $12,000. (This property had its roots in the American Revolution; it was part of the land owned by Old Tennent Church that was the site of the Battle of Monmouth.) Finally, the Sickles farm and the William Denise farm—both on the Colt's Neck Road—were sold.

MONMOUTH COUNTY HISTORICAL ASSOCIATION. Located at 70 Court Street, this building houses the most comprehensive collection of information on Monmouth County. (Courtesy of Randall Gabrielan.)

CARNEGIE LIBRARY. Home of the Freehold Public Library, this building was financed by steel and oil magnate Andrew Carnegie. (Courtesy of Randall Gabrielan.)

In January 1928, after more than 40 years of farming and canning in Freehold, Joseph Brakeley reorganized his company, named it Brakeley's Incorporated of Milford, Delaware, and moved it to that state. His farm machinery and equipment were sold at auction in February. The property on Manalapan and Bowne Avenues was acquired in 1941 by another enterprising company—A&M Karagheusian Rug Mill—for storage. Finally, in 1958, Monmouth County acquired the site. Today it is used as a county maintenance yard.

In the mid-1800s, two Armenians, Arshag and Miran Karagheusian, inherited a textile import business from their father, which he had begun in 1818. In the late nineteenth century, the Turkish government experienced a period of unrest and the brothers moved to the United States. They brought their company with them and began importing canary seed and mocha coffee. This business grew, but they decided to switch their import product to Oriental rugs. In 1899, the first shipments arrived in New York, where the Karagheusians set up a plush showroom to entice wealthy customers. The showroom was designed by Tiffany Studios and proved a big hit with affluent New Yorkers. Before long, wealthy Americans throughout the country decorated their homes with the Karagheusian-imported Oriental rugs.

In 1904, Arshag and Miran made another important decision to manufacture the rugs here in America. They chose a building at the intersection of Jackson and Center Streets in Freehold to set up a factory and traveled to England to purchase 60 Brussels and Jacquard Wilton power looms. Then they hired weavers to run the looms and brought all back to Freehold, where they manufactured some of the finest Oriental rugs in America. These Oriental-type or American Oriental rugs were featured in the Sears Catalog under the names of Mindora, Karaban, and Shah-Abbas. The Karagheusian brothers constantly searched for a better product and in the 1920s, began using new technology that added a soft patina to carpets. These improved rugs were labeled with the name Gulistan Deluxe.

Another early industrial company to make Freehold its home was the Stokes Brothers Manufacturing Company. On December 21, 1888, five members of the Stokes family—William H., Philip S., James, John H., and Samuel S.—along with George A. Hulett, George H. and Thomas A. Ward, Frank B. Conover, and William S. Throckmorton signed papers of incorporation. The owners started the small manufacturing operation at 15 Bannard Street adjacent to the Freehold & Jamesburg Agricultural Railroad with $40,000 in assets. It opened for business on December 24, 1888. The original brick building was built in the 1880s and 1890s with an addition made in 1915. Auxiliary buildings were constructed between 1890 and 1915. Stokes Brothers manufactured horse rasps, files, and various types of machinery.

As the industrial revolution and the automobile took hold in American society, the need for horseshoe supplies diminished substantially and Stokes's business began to decline. Further, the horseshoe supplies manufactured by the Stokes brothers on a small scale could also be mass-produced faster in much larger factories. By the early twentieth century, Stokes Brothers Manufacturing Company became another piece of Freehold history. Today, a portion of the Stokes building is listed on the Monmouth County Historic Sites Inventory.

John H. Bawden and Gilbert Combs established an iron foundry in 1856. Several references to the company are found in contemporary photographs and newspaper articles. At times it was referred to as J.H. Bawden & Company, at other times as Combs & Bawden Foundry, and at still other times as Freehold Iron Foundry. The company's short history is not well documented, but it operated until 1890.

The nineteenth century was a time of enormous change in industry. Brakeley's cannery, Stokes's file and rasp factory, and A&M Karagheusian's rug mill helped advance Freehold's participation in America's transformation from an agricultural society to an industrial center. These companies reached their zeniths by the early twentieth century, but by the time World War II began, they moved out of the area of their births and into the pages of Freehold's history.

The pace of life also moved quicker in the later part of the nineteenth century. The residents of Freehold demanded their own public utilities and that demand was met, starting in 1883. The first telephone switchboard was installed at the home of Irving Dudley at Marcy and Parker Streets on June 12 of that year. Six years later, in 1889, the first light switch was turned on and electric service began. The following year, the water works began operation. Throughout the late nineteenth and early twentieth centuries, the water supply and sewerage were improved. Electricity was used for more than just the lighting that had been provided by candles and gas. Telephone and electric service became a normal commodity. Coal was no longer the primary source for heating homes and businesses; natural gas was a cleaner, more efficient fuel. The hollow sound of heels clopping on plank sidewalks was replaced by the crisper sound made on concrete. Roads were no longer blemished with bothersome mud puddles, as macadam paved their surfaces.

Dr. William Hepburn was a well-respected physician who served on the township committee from the late 1800s to the turn of the century. He was Governor Joel Parker's personal physician after the Civil War. Dr. Hepburn built a home in 1885 on Monument Street that he used as his medical office and residence. The Queen Anne–style home has a polygonal porch, stained glass windows, and inlaid parquet floors characteristic of that period. It is operated today as a historic bed and breakfast.

Freehold's Jewish community formed the Freehold Hebrew Association in 1894. They built their first Synagogue, Congregation Agudath Achim, between 1911 and 1916 on the corner of First and Center streets. As the Jewish community grew, they needed a larger synagogue and built one on the corner of Broad and Stokes Streets in 1957.

As the nineteenth century drew to a close, a group of Monmouth County residents realized the need to preserve its history. Accordingly, in 1898, the Monmouth County Historical Association was founded. Its early collections were housed in the Red Bank Public Library. Then in 1931, the present-day building at 70 Court Street in Freehold Borough was designed by J. Hallam Conover (1897–1972) and built on property donated by David Vanderveer Perrine. Today, the association is an excellent source of historical information on Freehold as well as all the communities of Monmouth County.

Freehold had a subscription library by the turn of the twentieth century thanks to the efforts of the King's Daughters, a charitable and social organization associated with the Baptist church. They established the library on January 6, 1900 with 500 volumes. In December 1901, a fire damaged the collection and Miss Marian Laird, who chaired the library committee of the King's Daughters, led a campaign to rebuild the library. Miss Laird wrote an appeal to steel and oil magnate Andrew Carnegie. Carnegie agreed to donate $10,000 if the township agreed to raise $1,100 per year to support the library. The township voted in favor of this arrangement and the library was built at 28 East Main Street. Once the building was completed, however, the township had no money left for sidewalks. They again appealed to Carnegie, who graciously donated another $10,000 for this purpose. The library opened in 1904 with about 2,400 volumes. Miss Julia Combs was its first librarian.

The Freehold Merchants Association printed a postcard-sized fact sheet about Freehold c. 1901. The card boasted of Freehold's amenities and pointed out that free land was offered to anyone looking for a possible factory site. Printed on the front of the card, along with an image of the Monmouth County courthouse, were the following words:

BRAKELEY CANNING COMPANY, c. 1921. The man standing beside the tractor with his hands in his pockets is Joseph Brakeley, owner. Standing in the back are John Powers, Hugh Mcgowan, and William W. Smock. (Courtesy of Freehold Public Library.)

Freehold, The County Seat of Monmouth
We are proud of Freehold, "The Gateway to the Seashore"

A Beautiful Place to Live in.
A Good Place to Manufacture in.
A Good Place to do Business in.
A Good Place to Invest in.
We Invite You to Come to
Freehold, N.J.

According to the back of the card, Freehold's population was 5,000. Seven hundred students attended public schools with one hundred sixty students in each of the parochial and military schools. Amenities included a 500-seat theatre, a fire department with 150 firemen, five large hotels, two steam railroads (the Pennsylvania Railroad and the Central Railroad of New Jersey), eight churches, one hundred fifty businesses, a public water system, and an excellent mail system. Freehold produced $1,375,000 in manufactured products. Its total assessed real estate value was $1,802,719 and total value of personal property was $749,140. The tax rate for the town and township combined was $17.48 per $1,000. The Merchant Association's description of Freehold was simply, "Freehold is the county seat of Monmouth and located in the center of a thriving agricultural neighborhood, which has been steadily growing for the past five years."

The "excellent mail system" included mail stops at the American Hotel, the Union House, and Rescarrick Moore Smith's tavern. Mail was loaded onto a stagecoach at 5:00 a.m. every day except Sunday at the American Hotel. It was then brought to Keyport and loaded onto the steamship *Cinderella,* bound for New York. The steamer returned with a new load of mail and the cycle continued. Another mail stop was set up for 6:00 a.m. at the Union House, owned at the time by Nathaniel Rue. This load was taken to Smith's Tavern in Hightstown and then loaded onto the Camden & Amboy Railroad, bound for New York, Philadelphia, Trenton, Bordentown, Burlington, and Camden. Mail was picked up on the return trips and brought back to Smith's tavern and the Union House. Stagecoaches also carried mail from Freehold to Tuckerton with stops in between.

The industrial revolution brought about change in Freehold. The community invited businesses and industry to make Freehold their home. Soon bicycles, rugs, horse-shoeing equipment, and other items were being manufactured or processed there. The residents enjoyed the comfort and convenience of gas, electricity, and telephone service. In the midst of progress came destruction by fire, but the people of Freehold survived the devastation and continued moving forward. As they did, they did not forget their past. They provided a haven for historic records that still exists today.

MAIN STREET. This view looks west from Court Street in Freehold Borough. (Courtesy of Freehold Public Library.)

11. FREEHOLD IN THE TWENTIETH CENTURY

In the twentieth century, technology continued to progress at a rapid pace. The tracking and recording of weather was greatly improved. According to the National Weather Service, Freehold has an average 178-day growing season from April 23 through October 18. Average precipitation is 46 inches. Record temperatures were reached in July 1936, when the thermometer soared to 106 degrees Fahrenheit and in February 1934, when they plummeted to 20 degrees below zero Fahrenheit. Freehold experienced a drought from September 1961 through August 1966. The record for maximum snowfall in one month was 26 inches in December 1957. The maximum snowfall in one season was 66 9/10 inches during the winter of 1957–1958. One of the worst snowstorms hit on March 1, 1914. Freehold also experienced a tornado in 1900 and several ice storms, one of the worst in 1902.

The residents of Freehold faced several health crises in the early twentieth century, beginning with a rabies epidemic in 1910. The police department issued orders to shoot any stray animals on sight. In the early 1900s, the United States also faced a polio epidemic. Shortly before the 1916 school year began, Freehold was struck and school openings were postponed. The epidemic took the life of only one Freehold Township resident, but changed the lives of many more.

The population of Freehold in 1912 was 5,100, including a small percentage of non-English speaking immigrants. The value of taxable property was $2,956,800. Postal service, sewer, water, telegraph, telephone, electric service, and a volunteer fire department were available to residents. Central National Bank, First National Bank, National Freehold Banking Company, and one building and loan association served the financial needs of the community. There were eight established churches. Two public schools (one grammar school and one high school), a parochial school, and two private military schools educated the children. Two railroads—the Pennsylvania Railroad and Central Railroad of New Jersey—had stations in the center of town, providing freight and passenger service at a reasonable cost. The Freehold Merchants Association functioned as the board of trade. Manufacturing was encouraged on suitable land. Some parcels were

WEST MAIN STREET. This view of Freehold Borough is from the turn of the twentieth century, before the roads were paved. (Courtesy of Randall Gabrielan.)

available free of charge, while other more prime lots were sold at reduced prices. Financial assistance was available to anyone who could prove themselves capable of managing a factory.

The principle industries of Freehold in the early twentieth century were: J.H. Bawden & Company, an iron foundry employing 26 people; Joseph Brakeley's cannery, which employed 400 people; Sigmund Eisner Company, a shirt factory, with 75 employees; A&M Karagheusian Rug Mill, which employed 228 ; Charles Sandberg & Brother, underwear manufacturers, employing 50; and Stevens Wilbur Company, maker of men's shirts, with 57 employees. The center of Freehold developed into a town revolving around business activities on Main Street, while the surrounding area was still mostly farmland. The farmers of Freehold produced wheat, rye, potatoes, asparagus, fruit, and berries. A large part of the farming operation was dedicated to raising poultry. As the township developed, its citizens talked of a new form of municipal government.

Freehold had adopted the township form of municipal government with the passage of the Township Act of 1798. In 1869, the Town of Freehold incorporated and its boundary was similar to that of today's Borough of Freehold. Although it was a separate entity, the township retained the responsibility of collecting taxes and distributing revenues. The people in the Town of Freehold paid their taxes, but when it came time to receive revenues, they were not satisfied with the portion given them by the township. As a result, the town looked to other options to establish their own, independent municipal government.

Towards the end of the nineteenth century, a new form of municipal government was created by the New Jersey state legislature. Senator William H. Hendrickson and Assemblymen George J. Ely, William H. Bennett, and Arthur Wilson represented Monmouth County in the 102nd session in 1878. On April 5, the first general Borough Act was passed, providing for a borough form of municipal government. The size of a borough was limited to 4 square miles and the population was not to exceed 5,000. A mayor and six councilmen were to be elected annually on the first Tuesday of October at 2:00 p.m. The council was empowered to perform a list of duties, including enacting laws, preventing fast driving, issuing licenses, preventing animals from running wild, appropriating money, and assessing and collecting taxes.

At the time, the village of Freehold was discussing changing its form of government. However, not until a revised Borough Act was passed in 1897, did the plan seem appropriate for Freehold. This new law allowed boroughs to assess and collect taxes independent of the township from which the borough seceded. The 1897 revision provided more power and more elected officials to the borough. The Board of Chosen Freeholders of Monmouth County discussed the pros and cons of a borough government for several more years. Then, on August 22, 1917, it adopted a resolution to annex sections of Freehold township to the

EAST MAIN STREET. This view looks down East Main Street in Freehold Borough. (Courtesy of Freehold Public Library.)

town of Freehold and to incorporate the newly designated area as a borough. The new area included the current town and portions of the township from the outskirts of South Street and Main Street, the Texas section and part of the West End section. Two years later, on a Monday night in January 1919, the residents of Freehold met at the municipal building to discuss this resolution.

The *Monmouth Democrat* reported that there was some opposition to the proposal, mainly from residents of the sections that were being considered for annexation. Their main concern was that, as part of the borough, they would be required to pay higher taxes, but would get nothing in return. The debate waged on, but in the end, those present agreed to the annexation and adopted the following resolution:

> *Resolved:* That the town of Freehold be incorporated under a borough government, and that the proposed boundaries of the new borough be adopted and the territory therein annexed to the present town under the title of Borough of Freehold.

The Board of Chosen Freeholders presented the resolution to the state legislature, who approved it on July 5, 1919. The newly-annexed areas and the

MAIN STREET. *This view shows what Main Street looked like before the roads were paved. (Courtesy of Freehold Public Library.)*

Town of Freehold united under a borough form of government and became known as the Borough of Freehold. Under this new government, the borough maintained the status of Monmouth County Seat. A final section of Freehold Township joined the borough on September 7, 1926. This was to be the last split in the long history of division in Freehold Township.

The first mayor of the Borough of Freehold was William S. Holmes. The first council consisted of M. Henry Williams, Peter F. Runyun, Joseph E. DuBois, Peter Vredenburgh, Hycinth C. Levy, and Adrian E. Moreau. A borough clerk's office was established with the clerk's duties being generally to know every detail about the borough. In New Jersey, the borough clerk is considered one of the most important people in a municipal government. The first borough clerk was Harold McDermott, who served from 1919 until 1922.

The incorporation of the Borough of Freehold created one of only three such situations in Monmouth County in which a township surrounds a borough. The other two instances are in Farmingdale Borough, which is surrounded by Howell Township; and Englishtown Borough, which is surrounded by Manalapan Township. Effectively, Freehold Borough, the county seat, is an enclave surrounded by Freehold Township. This combination of township and borough has been the makeup of Freehold for the past 75 years. The Borough of Freehold has developed into a significant urban center with a wealth of eighteenth and nineteenth century buildings, including the old churches and many of the businesses that line Main Street.

According to Richmond's Freehold City Directory of 1922–1923, the population of Freehold Township rose from 2,234 in 1900 to 2,329 in 1910, then dropped to 1,498 in 1920. In the same timeframe, the population of Freehold Borough steadily rose from 2,934 in 1900 to 3,233 in 1910 to 4,768 in 1920. This was obviously a shift in the population due to the formation of the borough. Changes occurred in Monmouth County as well, as the new municipality carried on the role of county seat. County municipal offices had long been established in the hall of records in the center of Freehold, but the designation of the borough sparked new life in town. The county seat grew and prospered in Freehold Borough's early years, but by 1930, it fell victim to fire once again.

At 4:00 a.m. on April 19, 1930, the volunteer fire departments of Freehold and Englishtown responded to a fire alarm emanating from the courthouse. Later that day, at 2:30 p.m., Freeholders met to assess the damage and make repairs. One of them, a Mr. Polhemus, reported a preliminary estimate of the damage at $88,000. This was subdivided into $61,300 for the courthouse, $20,700 for furniture and fixtures, and $6,000 for the law library. He asked the board to approve architect Leon Cubberly to survey the damages and prepare plans to remodel the courthouse. He also asked the board to allocate $25,000 for emergency repairs. The board complied and work began shortly thereafter.

A precursor to today's business-to-business directories was Polk's Freehold Directory. Polk's provided an alphabetical list of names and contact information for Monmouth County businesses, plus additional demographics. The

*MONMOUTH
COUNTY
COURTHOUSE
FIRE, APRIL 19,
1930. The
courthouse
sustained
$88,000 in
damage due to this
fire. (Courtesy of
Freehold Public
Library.)*

1937–1938 directory listed the form of government as "Councilmanic (borough)." According to the directory, the borough was 1.5 square miles in total area and rose 190 feet above sea level. Taxes were assessed at $4.11 per $100, with the total assessed value for the entire borough at $6,194,346. It had two banks and one trust company, and its major manufactured products were rugs, carpets, clothing, and iron.

Several drug stores were established in Freehold. Rosell's Drug Store was on Throckmorton and Main Streets. On the eastern side of town, Stephen Wood's Drug Store was located on South and Mechanic Streets. In the center of town at 1 Courthouse Square was Eugene F. DuBois Drug Store, which eventually moved to Court Street.

Two weekly newspapers were published. Travelers could stay in one of two hotels, and the Pennsylvania Railroad and Central Jersey Railroad provided transportation throughout the state. Freehold Borough's children had a choice of five public schools, one parochial school, and one military academy. Twenty-five of the thirty miles of streets were paved—mostly with concrete, which had surfaced as the material of choice around the 1920s. The 6,894 residents were serviced by 20 sewers, 6 pieces of motorized fire-fighting equipment, and 5 policemen. Gas was supplied to 1,400 customers, while water and electric was supplied to 1,750 customers.

A peculiar aspect of travel in New Jersey is the use of traffic circles, and Freehold had its own example. On October 1, 1938, the Freehold traffic circle opened at the intersection of Routes 9 and 33 near Freehold Raceway. In the late twentieth century, the concept of traffic circles was challenged and most circles throughout the state were slated for destruction. For Freehold, this elimination was completed in 1990 when the roads around the newly-completed Freehold Raceway Mall were repaved to accommodate the anticipated increase of vehicle traffic. This project was part of the deal with Wilmorite, Inc. when they negotiated the mall construction. The road work cost Wilmorite $13.5 million.

Freehold Borough is home to one of the oldest diners in the area. The Freehold Grill, located at 59 East Main Street, has been serving basic diner food since about 1946. It is designed with the restaurant section facing East Main Street in Freehold Borough with a residence attached to the back of the building. Jerry O'Mahoney of Elizabeth, New Jersey built the diner.

BATHING AT LAKE TOPANEUMS. *This postcard shows swimmers enjoying the lake in the early twentieth century. (Courtesy of Monmouth County Historical Association Library and Archives.)*

By 1948 another large company, Nestle's, moved to Freehold. The company was lured to the area by its close proximity to prime markets in the eastern United States and by its easily-accessible water supply, an important factor in the production of coffee products. Area residents also were willing to provide the manpower needed to make the company a productive commercial force in the community. Sometime in the 1970s, Nestle expanded its operation with an addition to the plant. Today, Nestle is the only plant in America that produces freeze-dried coffee and is one of Freehold's major employers.

On April 7, 1962, fire once again devastated a large portion of Freehold along East Main Street. Nine stores, their upstairs apartments, and offices were destroyed, as was the lobby of the Strand movie theater. Two years later, on February 26, 1964, fire again destroyed several stores and a bowling alley on East Main Street.

Two historical associations, Monmouth Battlefield Association, Inc. and Monmouth County Historical Society, prompted the State of New Jersey to buy land and develop a park to commemorate the Revolutionary War Battle of Monmouth. In 1968, the Division of Parks, Forestry, and Recreation of the Department of Conservation and Economic Development agreed to the project as a means of preserving and perpetuating the historical significance of the site. The land was in near-natural condition and could be used to recapture the colonial landscape. During a time when Americans became increasingly aware of the need to preserve open space amongst rapid development, the State of New Jersey acquired approximately 130 acres from the owners of Battleview Orchards using Green Acres funds (state money set aside for land preservation) and created Monmouth Battlefield State Park. The 1,800-acre park has been designated a National Historic Landmark. It is located in Manalapan, 1 mile west of Freehold Borough, 25 miles east of Trenton, and 40 miles south of Newark. Route 33, Wemrock Road, County Route 522, and Route 9 border the historic park.

The park's visitor's center includes historic displays and a gift shop where patrons can purchase books and items relative to America's colonial period, the American Revolution, and the Civil War. Visitors can tour the Hedgerow, where American and British soldiers engaged in bloody hand-to-hand fighting; Perrine Ridge, where Molly Pitcher served the revolutionary cause; the Craig House; and the site of Civil War Camp Vredenburgh. Today, the Friends of Monmouth Battlefield have taken on the role of interpreters and protectors of the history of the battlefield. Since the group was created in 1990, it has been involved in several significant historical projects ranging from land acquisition to historical research to reprinting and publication of books, maps, and documents related to the Battle of Monmouth.

In the 1960s, Freehold developed into a heavily-populated area whose residents were hard-pressed for medical services. Accordingly, efforts were made to organize a local hospital and eliminate the transporting of patients to other area hospitals, such as Fitkin Hospital in Neptune (now known as Jersey Shore Medical Center), Monmouth Memorial Hospital in Long Branch (now known as

Monmouth Medical Center), or Riverview Hospital in Red Bank. Fundraising events were held throughout the 1960s, and on December 1, 1968, a groundbreaking ceremony took place at the site of what had been the Donovan farm on Route 537.

Construction occurred over 3 years and on September 21, 1971, the Greater Freehold Area Hospital opened its doors. The hospital had 120 beds and was equipped to provide fundamental medical care. With continued population growth, the hospital required expansion within just a few years. By 1977, $2 million were spent on the addition of the North Tower, a larger emergency room, a short-stay unit, a high-tech critical care unit, and 40 additional beds. The 1980s saw a trend toward wellness care and in 1981, the Greater Freehold Area Hospital opened such a center to provide area residents with laboratory, rehabilitation, and mental health services. More upgrades and additions were made throughout the 1980s. Hospice, Continuing Care, Ambulatory Care, and Convenience Care Centers were added to the fundamental services.

In 1990, Greater Freehold Area Hospital changed its name to CentraState Medical Center. Today, CentraState Healthcare System is one of Monmouth

THE MONMOUTH TITLE & MORTGAGE GUARANTY COMPANY, 1928. The company was located on the northeast corner of Court House Square and Main Street in the borough. This drawing was used for their prospectus. (Courtesy of Monmouth County Historical Association Library and Archives.)

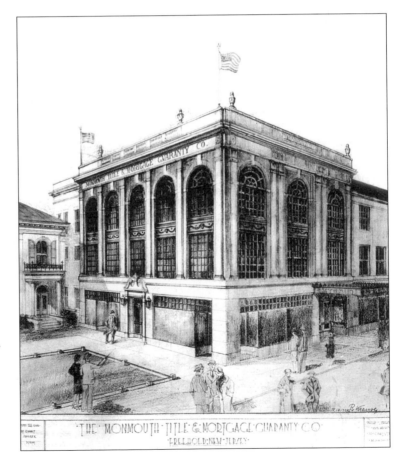

A&M KARAGHUESIAN RUG MILL. This shows the Burling Department of the rug mill around 1910. (Courtesy of Monmouth County Historical Association Library and Archives.)

County's largest employers and provides health care to over 35,000 patients annually. Along with the growth of the hospital, other medical service providers have sprung up in offices and satellite centers around CentraState.

Brockway Glass was one of the major industries to open in the township after World War II. In 1956, the Pennsylvania company began construction of a plant on the site of William N. Thompson's farm and began manufacturing glass the following year. In the 1970s, business boomed and the company expanded its plant. By the 1990s, Brockway Glass was a major employer with over 650 workers. Unfortunately, the boom was short-lived and the plant closed its doors in October 1991.

Another major industry that moved to Freehold Township was 3M (Minnesota Mining & Manufacturing Company). In 1957, it began manufacturing magnetic products and within 3 years constructed a larger facility. The new, 115,000-square-foot plant was located on a 30-acre parcel of land and operated for 26 years. Then, in 1986, 3M closed its doors and moved out of Freehold, leaving hundreds unemployed.

Even while promoting industrial development, Freehold residents proved themselves dedicated to land preservation. Approximately 6,000 acres—representing 25 percent of the total area of the township and borough—were dedicated to farmland, parks, and undeveloped land. In 1961, the Monmouth County Park System was created to address the open space and recreation needs of its residents. Baysholm Tract, East Freehold Park, Turkey Swamp Park, and the Durand Tract were all opened. The last is maintained by Freehold Township; Monmouth County Park system manages the other facilities, all located in Freehold Township. Each provides recreational space to the residents of both the township and the borough.

As awareness of environmental issues heightened during the twentieth century, several locations throughout New Jersey were listed as superfund sites. Such areas needed to be cleaned up and restored to their natural condition, a multi-million dollar proposal. One site, the Lone Pine Landfill, is located in Freehold. Its 57 acres are part of a 144-acre piece of land surrounded by the Manasquan River, a leaf-composting facility, and forested wetlands. From 1959 to 1979, over 17,000 drums of chemical waste, municipal refuse, seepage, and bulk liquid chemical wastes were deposited, severely contaminating the ground water. Turkey Swamp Fish and Wildlife Management Area is located within 1,000 feet of the landfill. After environmental impact studies were conducted, the site was placed on the Environmental Protection Agency's National Priorities List in September 1983. It has since been cleaned up. However, the EPA determined in 1999 that the site needs to be maintained and monitored until restored to its natural condition.

In the mid-1980s, a civic group with representatives from the Borough of Freehold organized as the Freehold Center Partnership. The group began a renovation project aimed at advancing downtown economic, cultural, and commercial development. The idea was to update the older, center part of the borough and promote the specialty shops, services, and restaurants around and along Main Street. Local businesses, as well as the various county government agencies that make their home in the county seat, have supported the project. The town center has received a facelift, from widened repaved sidewalks, to the renovation of the old Karagheusian Rug Mill, to the rebuilding of the Liberty Street Park. Hundreds of volunteers banded together to work on the park in August 2001.

One of the most popular events sponsored by the Freehold Center Partnership and the Western Monmouth County Chamber of Commerce is Kruise Night. On the last Thursday of each month between May and September, Main Street is blocked off and families from all over join in the fun and festivities. Classic cars and motorcycles park along Main Street for passersby to admire. Nonprofit organizations set up tables with information about their causes. Shops and restaurants are open and the atmosphere is filled with the sights, sounds, and smells of a street fair. While Kruise Night entertains, its main purpose is to serve the members of the community who are less fortunate. During the event, food is collected at designated drop-off points throughout Freehold Borough. The collected items are then distributed to those in need through the local food pantry. Kruise Night is testament to the community-mindedness of the residents of Freehold.

The A&M Karagheusian Rug Mill expanded between 1915 and 1930. In 1905, it employed 150 people. That number doubled by 1918 and by 1940, the Freehold rug factory employed over 1,700. Oriental-type rugs were shipped to 10,000 retailers and sold through 16 sales offices. In these years of expansion, a creel boy earned 22.5¢ an hour making different kinds of knots and assisting the weaver. After an apprenticeship of seven or eight years, a creel boy could become a weaver and earn substantially more money. Another job was that of a skein winder, who put wool on the bobbins.

One of the main concerns for the Karagheusians was the safety of their employees. In 1939, Arshag and Miran trained two men from each department to handle any medical emergencies on the premises. A bell signaled such an emergency and trained employees responded to the scene to handle the crisis. The employees remained on the payroll while answering the calls. After two years of practicing emergency procedures at the rug mill, some of the trained employees started a first aid squad to serve the residents of Freehold. Fourteen men joined together in this venture: Robert Bennett, David Blackburn, Pat Ciccerone, Joseph Donovan, Ennis Estelle, Ralph Hanson, Sidney Jackson, Warren McNinnie, Warren Oakerson, Robert Searby, Edward Spuler, Martin Wagner, Lawrence Willis, and Charles Witcavich. In September 1941, with a 1933 Cadillac LaSalle ambulance and some help from Karagheusian in the form of donated building space and a parking lot, the group organized the Freehold First Aid and Emergency Squad.

Over the years, the squad members faced some difficulties, but kept up service to the community through fundraising and sometimes dipping into their own pockets to buy supplies and equipment. In 1947, they purchased a lot with a house on Spring Street. By the 1950s, the squad increased its membership and had a fleet of three ambulances. The squad showed its commitment to the community by expanding its scope of service and creating the Freehold First Aid Cadet Corps in 1964. This organization was for teens interested in learning about emergency service. Squad members Woodrow "Chubby" Lykes and James Sweetman advised the cadets.

The founding of the Freehold First Aid Squad came about just before World War II. After the war started, the Karagheusians made a critical decision to stop manufacturing rugs and instead produce duck cloth for the war effort. After the war, the factory returned to the business of rug making and in 1949, built a new mill in Freehold. By 1957, the Karagheusians experienced labor disagreements and strikes. Rug production was phased out in the Freehold factory and moved to North Carolina. This move was completed in 1962, ending the history of A&M Karagheusian Rug Mill in Freehold.

After the mill moved out of Freehold, its factory building sustained damage from a fire in 1990. Then in 1998—as communities throughout the United States became increasingly aware of the needs of senior citizens, such as housing—the New Jersey Department of Community Affairs and the New Jersey Housing and Mortgage Finance Agency approved plans to renovate the building into 200 senior apartments. Over $9 million was loaned to the development company to renovate the structure. In May 2001, the former rug mill was

WATER WORKS. In 1890, the residents of Freehold began receiving water supplied by this pumping station. (Courtesy of Freehold Public Library.)

reopened. The renovated building includes 104 affordable rental units and 98 apartments for senior citizens. Its ground floor houses commercial offices, the Freehold Borough Police Station, the Freehold Borough Municipal Court, and a YMCA teen center. The Karagheusian Rug Mill, once a major employer in Freehold, was reclaimed by its residents. However, its former existence was not forgotten. The decline of the mill—and so many other downtown properties—was immortalized in a song entitled "My Hometown," by Freehold's favorite son, Bruce Springsteen.

Douglas and Adele Springsteen became the parents of Bruce Frederick on September 23, 1949. Springsteen's ancestors were among the original Dutch settlers of New Jersey. They fought in the American Revolution and Civil War. Douglas worked at the rug mill and at M&Q Plastics on Bannard Street. Adele worked in the Lawyer's Title Building on West Main Street. The Springsteens were a typical working-class family. They lived in a small home on Randolph Street until Bruce was about six years old. They then moved several blocks away to 39 1/2 Institute Street when St. Rose of Lima Church bought the property on Randolph Street, razed the home, and paved a parking lot. The Springsteens lived on Institute Street for seven years until 1962, when they moved a few blocks away to South Street.

In 1963, Bruce graduated 8th grade from St. Rose of Lima School and went on to Freehold Borough High School. During high school, he was a member of several rock bands: The Castiles, Earth, Steel Mill, and Dr. Zoom and the Sonic Boom. Local lore says that during a period of renovation at Freehold Borough High School, a tree under which Bruce supposedly sang was targeted for removal. When the students learned of this, they protested. An agreement was reached to preserve a limb from the hallowed tree in the school library.

After he graduated in 1967, Springsteen spent a short time at Ocean County College, but decided that music was his true love. He lived in Freehold Borough until he was 18 years old.

In 1972, Springsteen signed a contract with Columbia Records and began his musical career with the E Street Band. A year later, they released *Greetings from Asbury Park*. Although the album originally had poor sales, Springsteen continued to record. Ten months later, he released *The Wild, the Innocent & The E Street Shuffle*. This album had similarly disappointing sales, but people—particularly a music critic from *Rolling Stone*—started to take notice. Jon Landau saw the band perform in May 1974 and reported: "I saw rock 'n' roll's future and its name is Bruce Springsteen." The rest is history.

A&M KARAGHUESIAN RUG MILL. This aerial view is of the rug mill before 1950. The mill left town by 1962 and the farmland in the background has long since been developed. (Courtesy of Monmouth County Historical Association Library and Archives.)

Throughout his career, Springsteen has done much to advance causes in which he believes. On September 22 and 23, 1978, he performed at the historic MUSE concert at Madison Square Garden in New York, to protest the proliferation of nuclear weapons. In 1985, he participated in the USA For Africa production of *We are the World* and Artists United Against Apartheid's *Sun City*. He supported the Human Rights Now tour for Amnesty International in 1988.

In November 1996, Springsteen played to an audience of 1,300 at St. Rose's gymnasium to benefit the parish center renovations. The center provides services to the Hispanic community in Freehold Borough. The same month, he performed in a charity show at Paramount Theatre in Asbury Park. On January 31, 1998 he played the "Jon Bon Jovi & Friends" benefit for the family of Sergeant Patrick King, a police officer from neighboring Long Branch killed in the line of duty. Three months after the benefit for Sergeant King's family, Springsteen suffered his own loss. Douglas Springsteen died on April 26, 1998 in Belmont, California. The funeral was held at St. Rose of Lima Church in Freehold.

On November 16, 1986, the *Asbury Park Press* ran an article claiming that Springsteen was "rock's most bootlegged artist." The article relates the 1979 lawsuit that Springsteen and Columbia Records brought against a notorious group of bootleggers from California. The bootlegging industry was stirred up when the Federal Bureau of Investigation seized and destroyed 12 tons of bootlegged tapes of live recordings of Springsteen shows. When the smoke settled from the lawsuit, Columbia Records released *Bruce Springsteen and the E Street Band Live/1975–1985*.

Springsteen is revered as Freehold Borough's favorite son, just as the lyrics of "My Hometown" have memorialized that town. In fact, fans are obsessed with the Boss's home. On January 7, 1988, the *Asbury Park Press* printed a photograph of a house at 40 Bellevue Avenue in Rumson with a caption that it was recently purchased by Springsteen.

On March 15, 1999, Springsteen was inducted into the Rock & Roll Hall of Fame in Cleveland, Ohio. He recorded "American Skin" in June 2000. Its controversial lyrics protest the shooting of an unarmed Bronx resident, Amadou Diallo, by New York City police officers. Like most Americans, Springsteen was shaken by the terrorist attacks of September 11, 2001. His response was a collection of songs, *The Rising*, released in July 2002—his first album since 1987.

The twentieth century was a time of growth and expansion in Freehold. The township's population soared from 3,233 in 1910, to 4,779 in 1960, to 13,115 in 1970, and to 19,202 in 1980. Today, the number of people in the township exceeds 30,000. In 75 years, the population of the borough grew from around 3,000 to over 11,000. The landscape has irreversibly changed from a rural setting to a suburban community.

Although there is some effort to preserve open space, development encroaches on every acre. What was once farmland and meadows has transformed into developments of homes and commercial buildings. Families from busy cities moved into the suburbia called Freehold. The construction of the shopping mall in 1990 caused a shift in the commercial center from Main Street in Freehold Borough to the traffic nexus of Routes 9 and 33 in Freehold Township. What was once the naturally beautiful Lenapehoking is now a diverse suburban community flourishing with thousands of people and hundreds of commercial enterprises.

A&M KARAGHUESIAN RUG MILL. Here is a worker in the rug mill around 1950. (Courtesy of Monmouth County Historical Association Library and Archives.)

12. FREEHOLD IN THE NEW MILLENNIUM

Today, both Freehold Township and Freehold Borough are suburban communities with recreational opportunities, shopping, commercial amenities, close proximity to New York and Philadelphia, rich history, relatively low taxes, and a substantial school system. Several major companies employee thousands of residents. As of 2001, the list—provided by Monmouth County Economic Development—included the County of Monmouth, Freehold Raceway, Inc., CentraState Healthcare Systems, Foodarama Supermarkets, Inc., Norkus Enterprises, Inc., Nestle, IVC Industries, YMCA, and Applewood Estates. The Freehold Regional High School District operates high schools in Colts Neck, Freehold, Freehold Township, Howell, Manalapan, and Marlboro. Freehold Township Elementary School District consists of Clifton T. Barkalow School in the township and Joseph J. Catena School, Laura Donovan School, Dwight D. Eisenhower School, Marshall W. Errickson School, Richard C. Applegate School, and West Freehold School in the borough.

According to the Monmouth County Planning Board's 2000 demographic statistics, Freehold Township's population was 31,921, The board also reported the township's land area as 37 square miles. Freehold Borough's 2000 population was 11,562, with 3,695 households and a median family income of $68,843. The borough is comprised of 1.9 square miles and has easy access to major points in the region. Freehold is situated approximately 50 miles from New York City, 12 miles from the Jersey Shore, 90 miles from Atlantic City, and 70 miles from Philadelphia. A roadway network that began as Native American trails provides access to these areas and helps sustain Freehold as a commercial hub. Routes 9, 33, 79, and 537 are its main roads. Route 9 winds through the eastern part of New Jersey from Fort Lee in the north to Cape May in the south. It cuts a path through Freehold Township from the Manalapan border, just north of Monmouth Battlefield State Park, then circumvents the borough and leaves the township as it passes Route 524 near the northern border of Howell. Route 9 is lined with every kind of store imaginable including fast food and fine restaurants, car dealers, building warehouses, home furnishing outlets, office supply providers, florists,

BROADWAY AND EAST MAIN STREET, 2002. Today, the intersection of Route 79 (Broadway) and Route 537 (East Main Street) is paved and a memorial stands to those who sacrificed their lives in World War II. Compare with the photo on p. 125.

clothing stores, movie theaters, and super food stores. And at the crossroads of Routes 9, 33 and 537 is the largest shopping mall in Monmouth County, Freehold Raceway Mall.

Today, the one-lane and two-lane highways created at the turn of the twentieth century are being widened to accommodate the increase in population. Route 33 is a prime example of this process. For a large part of the roadway, Route 33 is a single-lane road connecting Trenton to Asbury Park. It is laid out east-to-west, crossing Freehold Township, intersecting Route 9, and skirting through the southeast portion of Freehold Borough. Route 33 Bypass has undergone a major renovation over the past few years. When completed, it will provide quicker access through Freehold, while the original roadway will remain a business route.

Route 79 starts in Keyport on the south Shore of Raritan Bay and traverses Matawan, Marlboro, the northern part of Freehold Township, and Freehold Borough—where it is known as Broadway. This road mainly consists of private homes and several small village shopping centers. When it reaches the borough, it joins Route 537 for several blocks through the center of town. It then runs south through the borough, splits from 537 at the southern end, and terminates at Route 33. Route 537 roughly follows the original Indian trail known as the Burlington Path and cuts across the township and through the borough connecting Camden

150

to Highlands. From south to north, Route 537 progresses in an easterly direction past some farmland. The landscape becomes less and less rural as it approaches the borough. In a few miles, signs of major development include a pizza restaurant, a nursery, a convenience store, several banks, a medical facility, numerous medical services buildings, Freehold Raceway Mall, and Maplewood Cemetery. At this point, the atmosphere takes on a village-like appearance as you approach the center of the borough and Route 537 becomes West Main Street.

West Main Street is dotted with large Victorian style homes and the old churches: First Presbyterian, First Baptist, and St. Peter's. The center of town is alive with people walking, driving, and cycling up and down West Main Street. Shops, cafes, fast food restaurants, and other commercial buildings house small companies and services. The Hall of Records stands at the corner of West Main and Court Streets on the original location of the Monmouth County courthouse and jail. Route 537 continues east out of the borough and just before entering the township once again, splits at Elks Point. The section of land that forms the V of the split between Routes 537 and 79 is a memorial to Freehold's fallen heroes of wars. The white crosses and American flags are symbols of Freehold's support of our country's ideals and the sacrifices made by residents of Freehold to uphold those ideals.

In the fall of the first year of the twenty-first century, those ideals were tested again as the United States was the victim of a horrific terrorist attack on

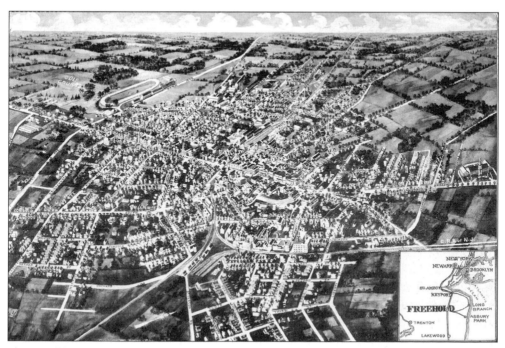

AERIAL VIEW OF FREEHOLD BOROUGH. This points out that at the time, the borough's population was 6,000. (Courtesy of Carl Beams.)

151

SEPTEMBER 11, 2001 MEMORIAL. Freehold Township erected this memorial to honor those who lost their lives in the terrorist attacks.

September 11, 2001. Hijacked planes were deliberately crashed into the Twin Towers in New York City and the Pentagon in Washington, D.C., while a third went down in a field near Pittsburgh, Pennsylvania. Thousands of Americans lost their lives and Freehold did not go unscathed. Several residents were victims. The people of Freehold Township, like those in other communities throughout the nation, joined together in their grief and built a memorial to the men, women, and children who died on that day. The memorial is located on the grounds of the municipal complex at the intersection of Schanck and Stillwells Corner Roads.

It consists of a pentagon-shaped monument enshrining pieces of the World Trade Center at its base. The marker with its encased fragments—which cannot be seen from the outside—symbolizes the final resting place of those who will never be recovered. A granite circle of 50 gold stars, one for each of the states, rests atop the monument and represents Ground Zero. Two miniatures of the Twin Towers carved in black granite are positioned atop the 50 gold stars. The five sides of the monument are inlaid with gold engravings that read: September 11, 2001, United Flight 93, United Flight 175, American Flight 11, and American Flight 77. The memorial is dedicated with the words:

It is with sadness that we see the need for a
    lasting memorial to our fallen countrymen.
It is with pride that we see a finished product
    worthy of those lost.
It is with gratitude we give our community for the outpouring
    of support and commitment to this project.
It is unity that we, the Freehold Township community,
    show to the country and the world.
It is deep understanding of the cost of American
    freedom and our way of life that we recognize.

To those taken from us at the hands
    of our enemies on September 11, 2001:

The thousands of innocent civilians,
    the hundreds of heroic rescue personnel
    from all branches of public service,
    the servicemen and women,
    and the countless heroes . . .

Americans heal, not by forgetting, but by remembering.
It is with this in mind that we dedicate this Memorial.

Thousands of years ago, the Lenape came to this region in search of a climate and food supply to sustain their lifestyle. Since that time, the people who made Freehold their home have been responsible for its progress and evolution. Freehold's story is as old as that of the United States. It has mirrored the revolutions, divisions, failures, accomplishments, and triumphs that have shaped our country. The harmonious existence of the borough within the township gives testament to the concept that, with a vision and the energy to work together, a wonderful community can evolve. Freehold's residents are responsible for its vitality today. Like the Lenape of long ago, they live in an area that is abundant with all the necessities to sustain a comfortable twenty-first-century lifestyle.

BIBLIOGRAPHY

Acts of the Sixty-Eighth General Assembly of the State of New Jersey, at the Session begun at Trenton on the Twenty-Fourth day of October, Eighteen Hundred and Forty-Three. Being the First Sitting. Freehold: Bernard Connolly, 1844.

Acts of the Seventy-First Legislature of the State of New Jersey and Third Session Under the New Constitution. Trenton, NJ: Phillips & Boswell, 1847.

Acts of the Seventy Second Legislature of the State of New Jersey and Fourth Under the New Constitution. Trenton, NJ: Phillips & Boswell, 1848.

Acts of the Ninety-Third Legislature of the State of New Jersey and Twenty-Fifth Under the New Constitution. New Brunswick, NJ: A.R. Speer, 1869.

Acts of the One Hundred and Forty-third Legislature of the State of New Jersey and Seventy Fifth Under the New Constitution. New Jersey: A.R. Speer, 1919.

Armstrong, William C. *Kerr Clan of New Jersey, Beginning with Walter Kerr of Freehold and Ending with Other Related Lists.* Salem, MA: Higginson Book Company, 1997.

Beekman, George C. and Edwin Salter. *Old Times in Old Monmouth.* Baltimore, MD: Genealogical Publishing Company, Inc., 1980.

Blair, Jeanette. *Freehold Township: The First 300 Years.* Freehold: Freehold Township Committee, 1993.

Cunningham, John T. *Railroads in New Jersey: The Formative Years.* New Jersey: Afton Publishing Company, Inc., 1997.

Ellis, Franklin. *History of Monmouth County, New Jersey.* Philadelphia: R.T. Peck & Company, 1885.

Dodyk, Delight W., Editor. *The Diary of Sarah Tabitha Reid, 1868–1873.* New Jersey: Monmouth County Historical Association, 2001.

Griffin, William L. *150 Years of Ministry 1838–1988. The First Presbyterian Church of Freehold, NJ.* Freehold: William L. Griffin, 1989.

Griffith, Lee Ellen. *Images of America: Freehold.* Charleston, SC: Arcadia Publishing, 1999.

Hodges, Graham Russell. *Slavery and Freedom in the Rural North: African Americans in Monmouth County, New Jersey, 1665–1865.* Madison, WI: Madison House, 1997.

Horner, William S. *This Old Monmouth of Ours.* Freehold: Morrow Brothers, 1932.

Kraft, Herbert C. *The Lenape Archaeology, History and Ethnography*. Newark, NJ: New Jersey Historical Society, 1986.

Martin, David G. *The Monocacy Regiment: A Commemorative History of the 14th New Jersey Infantry In the Civil War, 1862–1865*. Hightstown, NJ: Longstreet, 1987.

————. *"The Story of Molly Pitcher."* Hightstown, NJ: Longstreet, 2000.

New Jersey Historical Society. Proceedings. Vol. 65, No. 4. October, 1947.

Salter, Edwin. *A History of Monmouth and Ocean Counties, New Jersey*. Bayonne, NJ: E. Gardner & Sons, 1890.

Snyder, John P. *The Story of New Jersey's Civil Boundaries 1606–1968*. Trenton, NJ: Bureau of Geology and Topography, 1969.

Stillwell, Hamilton. *History of Old Tennent Church*. City, NJ: Guy Spencer, Grand Stand International, 1992.

Stryker, William S. *The Battle of Monmouth*. Princeton, NJ: Princeton University Press, 1927.

Symmes, Reverend Frank R. *History of The Old Tennent Church*, Second Edition. Cranbury, NJ: George W. Burroughs, 1904.

Wilbur, Lillian Lauler. *The Early Schools of Freehold and Vicinity 1667–1928*. Asbury Park, NJ: Schuyler Press, 1969.

INDEX

FIRST PRESBYTERIAN CHURCH MUTUAL IMPROVEMENT SOCIETY, FEBRUARY 1889. From left to right are: (first row) Morris, Dr. William E. Truex, possibly Andrew Chambers, Dr. William Hepburn, Theodore Morris Jr., Fred Parker, Samuel Coward, Reverend Henry G. Smith, Holmes Wheeler; (second row) Mrs. Mary Anna Schenck, Miss Elizabeth Barkalow, Miss Jennie Hamilton, Miss Annie Perrine, Miss Jennie Perrine, Mrs. Mary Walker; (third row) Mrs. William E. Truex, Miss Sara Parka, Mrs. William M. Hepburn, Mrs. Libby Mount, Mrs. Maggie Forman, Miss Lottie Arrowsmith, Miss Lizzie Forman, Mrs. Fred Parker; (fourth row) Mrs. Andrew Chambers, possibly Miss Julia Freeman, three unidentified women, possibly Mrs. Oakley, and Mr. Oakley. (Courtesy of Monmouth County Historical Association Library and Archives.)